THE MIAMI HEAT

AN ILLUSTRATED TIMELINE

Reedy Press
PO Box 5131
St. Louis, MO 63139, USA
reedypress.com

Library of Congress Control Number: 2025943539

ISBN: 9781681066080

Design by Craig Gartner and Linda Eckels
Front and back cover images courtesy of Getty Images
Images courtesy of Getty Images unless otherwise noted

Printed in Canada
25 26 27 28 29   5 4 3 2 1

DEDICATION

To my friends and family. To people who love basketball. To those who gave me the opportunity to be around this game. To my editors and colleagues. To the 518 and the 305 and every coach and teammate I've ever had.

And, above all else, to Linda, who makes all things possible and worthwhile.

CHAMPIONS

THE MIAMI HEAT

AN ILLUSTRATED TIMELINE

TIM REYNOLDS

REEDY PRESS

HEAT
14
HEAT
7

MIAMI HEAT

CONTENTS

2023

2024

2025

HEAT
6

HEAT
3

ACKNOWLEDGMENTS

TO THANK everyone who has helped me over these years, that would take another book.

I must thank the sports editors I've worked for at The Associated Press, including the late Terry Taylor (who saw something in me that I did not know was there), Michael Giarrusso, Howie Rumberg, Ricardo Zuniga and the editor who has put up with me for the longest, Oscar Dixon.

The sports media relations staffs around the league, particularly Tim Donovan, Rob Wilson, Michael Lissack, Nick Maiorana and Maddox Burnett with the Heat. Miami's front office—Pat Riley, Micky Arison, Nick Arison, Andy Elisburg and Erik Spoelstra—have always been more than fair, and I thank them for that and much more.

This is where I'll inevitably leave somebody out and feel awful about it, but here goes: Ken Tingley, Greg Brownell, the late Bob Goetz, Scott Goldman, John Allen, Melissa Hebert, Dave Lindquist, Matthew Crowley, Bill Callen, Tim Farkas, Rex Smith, Adam Yeomans, Tony Fiorentino for letting me think I could coach at Heat camp . . . I have learned more from all of you than I can ever explain.

To the NBA communications staff, thank you so much for being the best.

To our dear friends Harlan and Randy Selesnick, thank you for everything.

And above all else, there's the best editor I could ever have: my wife, Linda.

Without her, this book wouldn't have happened. Without her, this career wouldn't have happened.

Chris Bosh of the Miami Heat arrives at the 2010 ESPY Awards in Los Angeles

INTRODUCTION

MIAMI WAS a football town. It still is, thanks to the Miami Dolphins and Miami Hurricanes, but not exclusively . . . The Miami Heat changed that.

Go to any major city in the world, and you'll likely see Miami Heat jerseys on somebody's back. Dwyane Wade's No. 3 is iconic. LeBron James wore No. 6 in Miami. Chris Bosh wore No. 1.

Maybe they're of a newer vintage: Bam Adebayo's No. 13, Tyler Herro's No. 14, Jimmy Butler's No. 22.

The now-Miami, then–Florida Marlins have won a pair of World Series. The Florida Panthers won the Stanley Cup for the first time in 2024 and successfully defended the title in 2025. Baseball remains religious to the Latin population of South Florida, and hockey has made huge inroads thanks to the Panthers. And football is still football; it could certainly be argued that there is no spot on the planet that produces more elite talent than South Florida does.

But this is a basketball town, too.

The Heat made that reality, leaving an indelible impact on Miami and on the basketball world.

That's what happens when a team wins three NBA championships in the span of nine seasons, hoisting the Larry O'Brien Trophy in 2006, 2012, and 2013. The Heat have made the finals on four other occasions: 2011, 2014, 2020, and 2023. They've done it with iconic names on the court: Wade, James, Bosh, Shaquille O'Neal, Alonzo Mourning, Tim Hardaway. And there have been the off-the-court icons as well: Pat Riley changed everything when Micky Arison brought him in in 1995, and Arison wound up rightly enshrined in the Naismith Memorial Basketball Hall of Fame as well.

Kevin Love and Kyle Lowry were champions when they came to Miami and quickly became unforgettable parts of Heat lore. Gary Payton, the legendary guard, won his NBA title with the Heat. Jason Williams and Mario Chalmers always knew they would be championship-winning point guards; they fulfilled those legacies in Miami. And where else but the Magic City could a guy start his NBA career in the video room (and not know much about video, by the way) and become one of the game's greatest head coaches? Such is the tale of Erik Spoelstra, who will certainly be in the Hall of Fame himself one day.

The Heat, entering the 2025–26 season, have played about 3,300 games. That's almost 160,000 minutes of basketball, so there have been millions of moments. This book highlights a tiny sliver of them. It would be impossible to tell the entire story of the Heat in one book. But these moments and incredible photos hit at least some of the highlights, from how the Heat started to where they are now.

We hope you enjoy.

THE BEGINNING (BEFORE THE BEGINNING)

MIAMI'S FIRST NBA game was played long before the Heat were born.

This might have been one of the most important games in the city's NBA history: Washington Bullets 94, New Jersey Nets 92 in a preseason matchup on October 22, 1984.

The score didn't matter. The attendance did. They sold out the James L. Knight Center that night, fans grabbing all 5,000 tickets that were available in what was a clear message to the NBA: *We want basketball here*. And the league quickly took notice.

Miami was different then. There was nothing but football. The Florida Marlins were nearly a decade away from playing their first Major League Baseball game. Same goes for the NHL's Florida Panthers. Heat was an atmospheric condition in Miami, not a basketball team. The Miami Hurricanes were the reigning college football national champions at that time, and Dan Marino and the Miami Dolphins were the center of the city's sporting universe.

"Those fans tonight showed they want an NBA team here," Nets coach Stan Albeck said that night. "I'd like to see a team here."

Said Bullets coach Gene Shue: "I would love to see Miami with a team. Judging from the way the fans reacted tonight, they'd love to see it too."

The seeds were planted. NBA Commissioner David Stern wasn't there that night. He sent Gary Bettman in his place. (Bettman would go on to become commissioner of the NHL, someone who 40 years later would hand the Stanley Cup to the Florida Panthers.) South Florida was on its way.

Ted Arison, shown in 1994, was one of the visionaries who wound up bringing the Miami Heat to South Florida.

1986
MAY

MIAMI ANNOUNCES IT WANTS A TEAM

TED ARISON was not a big sports guy. Owning a professional basketball team was not exactly a top priority.

He owned Carnival Cruise Lines. He also loved Miami. That's why, when the idea of helping to bring a team to South Florida was initially presented to him, he didn't balk. He thought about it and realized that it could be a good thing for the region. Miami had the NFL's Dolphins and a major college football program in the Miami Hurricanes, but no other pro sports yet.

It was in May 1986 that Billy Cunningham and Zev Bufman detailed plans on how they wanted to bring a team to South Florida. Local officials approved plans for a new arena not long afterward. The application for an expansion franchise was officially filed with the NBA in June, and a few weeks after that Julio Iglesias and Lewis Schaffel joined the potential ownership group. Construction on the building, called Miami Arena, began in August. Things were happening.

Then in September, Ted Arison came aboard.

"I think Ted pulled a lot of things together," said David Stern, the NBA Commissioner at the time.

Ted Arison led the ownership group and was tapped to serve as Miami's representative on the NBA's Board of Governors. It became clear that Miami probably wouldn't have had much of a chance for approval without his involvement.

Micky Arison, Ted Arison's son, would say years later that, at first, he tried to discourage his father from the Heat deal. But in the end, he also saw the vision and noted that his father's financial investment, relative to his net worth, was small.

Let's just say it paid off.

NBA Commissioner David Stern speaks at a news conference in 1987.

THE NBA SELECTION

THE FIRST Miami vs. Orlando basketball game, officially, was on November 28, 1989. The Heat lost, 104–99.

But in reality, the first Heat vs. Magic battle was about two-and-a-half years earlier. And nobody lost.

It happened on April 22, 1987. Everybody presumed that, on that date, the NBA would announce that it was expanding to three cities. Minnesota and Charlotte were widely (and correctly) assumed to be two of those three. Miami or Orlando would be the other, most people thought. There was a vicious war of words between the two Florida cities, each trying to state its case as to why the NBA should come to them.

Some even expected the NBA to table the Miami vs. Orlando decision for six months, in part because arena construction in Central Florida was underway but a few months behind the pace of what was being built in South Florida.

Then came decision day, and the NBA couldn't decide. So, it simply added both cities.

"What do you do when you have two great applicants? You take them both," NBA Commissioner David Stern said that day at the Helmsley Palace Hotel in New York. "In this case, we felt that we had two great American cities that had met all the criteria for admission to the NBA."

The first employees of the Heat began showing up to work in early July 1987. Jeff Craney was an intern who arrived two-and-a-half hours early for his first shift. As of 2025, he still works for the Heat, one of a few who were with the franchise from the beginning and never left.

KAREEM ABDUL-JABBAR TO THE HEAT?

IT COULD HAVE HAPPENED.

HERE'S AN ironic twist: One of the first decisions that the Miami Heat made in their earliest days was to help the Los Angeles Lakers.

And that meant the Heat were helping Pat Riley . . . long before Pat Riley knew anything about Miami.

The Heat selected their very first players on June 23, 1988, in the expansion draft, taking Arvid Kramer, Billy Thompson, Fred Roberts, Scott Hastings, Jon Sundvold, Kevin Williams, Hansi Gnad, Darnell Valentine, Dwayne "Pearl" Washington, Andre Turner, Conner Henry, and John Stroeder. (Kramer, Roberts, Williams, Gnad, Valentine, Turner, Henry, and Stroeder never played for the Heat.)

That was quite a week for Kareem Abdul-Jabbar. On June 21, he and the Lakers beat Detroit in Game 7 of the NBA Finals for a second consecutive NBA championship. And one day later, while he and the Lakers were celebrating that crown, deals were struck by his club to ensure that neither Charlotte nor Miami would take him in the expansion draft.

The Lakers did not have Abdul-Jabbar on their eight-man protected list. He was turning 42 the following season and under contract for $3 million, so it seemed unlikely that the Hornets or Heat would take him. But just in case, the Lakers agreed to send Miami a second-round pick in 1992 to ensure that the Heat did not bring Abdul-Jabbar to South Florida.

The Heat turned that second-round pick into center Matt Geiger. He spent three seasons in Miami at the start of what became a 10-year NBA career.

Los Angeles Lakers coach Pat Riley and center Kareem Abdul-Jabbar discuss strategy during a game in 1988.

1988
JUNE 28

"WITH THE FIRST PICK . . ."

Syracuse center Rony Seikaly, shown in a game against Villanova, was one of the first Heat stars.

AROUND THE time that some people in and around Miami started thinking about the chances of the city getting an NBA team—four or so years before the Heat would wind up playing their first game—a kid named Rony Seikaly moved to the United States to see how good he could be at basketball.

Obviously, no one had any way of knowing how Seikaly and Miami would soon be connected.

On June 28, 1988, the Heat took part in their first NBA draft and had the ninth pick. Seikaly had just finished his college career at Syracuse, helping the then-Orangemen (the school's teams are just the Orange now) to the 1987 NCAA championship game against Indiana. He went to Madison Square Garden in New York hoping that he would soon be headed to Miami.

Here was the sentence from NBA Commissioner David Stern that Seikaly will never forget: "With the ninth pick in the draft and their first in the NBA, the Miami Heat select Ron Seikaly from Syracuse University."

Yes, Stern called him Ron. It could have been worse. Seikaly said the only thing he was worried about in Miami was getting mistaken for Miami Hurricanes quarterback Vinny Testaverde—and, in all seriousness, there was quite a facial resemblance between the two.

Testaverde wasn't 6-foot-11, however. So Seikaly was safe there.

Kevin Edwards was Miami's second first-round pick in that draft, going No. 20 overall. Miami got to select Edwards after striking a deal with Dallas for the Mavericks' first-round pick in exchange for not taking Bill Wennington, Uwe Blab, or Steve Alford in the expansion draft a few days earlier.

And with all that, the Heat were one step closer to opening night.

ANDY ELISBURG

A HEAT LIFER, A KEEPER OF THE CULTURE

ANDY ELISBURG has not worked for the Miami Heat for the entirety of his post-college life.

He took a day off first.

Yes, just one day. Not kidding.

And that's not even really true. Elisburg was already a Heat intern—"other duties as assigned" may as well have been his role, because he was involved wherever he was needed—while he was finishing college at St. Thomas University in Miami Gardens, Florida.

He graduated from college on a Monday. He took Tuesday off. He started his full-time work for the Heat on Wednesday. He never left.

"What we have here is something that makes us all really feel like we're part of something bigger than each of us as individuals, something that transcends what we are," Elisburg once said. "It isn't just a stepping stone. It isn't just another job. The Heat aren't just another team I root for. Heat basketball is a part of me."

These are the official titles that he's had with the Heat: intern, public relations assistant, Assistant Director of Public Relations, Director of Team Services and Information, Director of Team Operations, Vice President of Basketball Operations, Senior Vice President of Basketball Operations, Senior Vice President of Basketball Operations and Assistant General Manager, and, as of the end of the 2024-25 season, Senior Vice President and General Manager. His primary responsibility is managing the team's salary cap and ensuring that the team has the talent it needs to compete. He is also a proud keeper of the famed Heat culture.

"Culture is a standard," Elisburg said. "It's who we are."

Andy Elisburg started as an intern and eventually became one of the leaders of the Heat front office.

CHOOSING A STAFF

THE MIAMI HEAT had a name, they had some staff, and they had some players. The next step: landing a coach.

Ron Rothstein had come up the ranks the hard way. He was a high school coach in Westchester County, New York. Basketball was very much in his DNA; his uncle, Leo Gottlieb, at one time was the leading scorer in NBA history when he played for the New York Knicks in the league's inaugural season. (Technically, it was just for one day. Gottlieb became the scoring leader on November 2, 1946, the second day of the league's existence, and lost the title a day later.)

Rothstein got to the NBA in 1979 when well-known coach Mike Fratello recommended him to Hubie Brown, who was coaching the Atlanta Hawks. Brown hired Rothstein as a regional scout, then Fratello hired him as an assistant with Atlanta, and then Chuck Daly brought him to Detroit as part of his staff.

Rothstein had a reputation as a defensive-minded coach and as a teacher (which made sense, since he taught physical education to high schoolers for a few years). The Heat called and offered him the chance to be their first head coach, and Rothstein took over.

He officially became coach on July 11, 1988.

Expectations were understandably modest. "This is going to take time," Rothstein said when he got the job. He was right. Miami went 15–67, 18–64 and 24–58 in his three seasons, but kept getting better along the way. He planted the seeds and wound up staying in Miami for basically the rest of his basketball career as a WNBA coach for the Miami Sol, Heat assistant, and eventually a television and radio analyst for the Heat.

Ron Rothstein was the inaugural coach of the Heat, holding that role for the team's first three seasons.

1988
NOVEMBER 5

THE FIRST GAME CLIPPERS 111, HEAT 91

THE FANS showed up on a warm Saturday night in Miami—November 5, 1988—dressed more for an awards show in many cases than one typically would for a basketball game. Some men wore tuxedos, some women wore cocktail dresses and high heels. It wasn't by accident. The team actually encouraged fans to come to the first game in Heat history dressed in black tie.

Hey, it was a big deal.

Opening night for the Heat was a 20-point loss to the Los Angeles Clippers, 111–91. But that hardly mattered. The fans booed when actor Don Johnson mentioned fellow actor—and Los Angeles Lakers fan—Jack Nicholson in his pregame address, roared when Rory Sparrow made the first basket in franchise history and really went wild when Sylvester Gray threw down the first official dunk in a Heat game.

Pearl Washington was the first leading scorer, finishing the night with 16 points for Miami. It was the start of what most people realized would be a long and difficult road, but even a 20-point loss was something to celebrate that night in Miami.

It meant the NBA had finally, officially arrived. NBA Commissioner David Stern was there to see the first real game, saying he wished the Heat luck but—as was consistent to his nature during his 30 years overseeing the league—stopping well short of saying he was rooting for Miami. He was there to see a show, and Miami gave him one.

"The best thing about this game is that it's over with," Heat center Scott Hastings said that night.

Some fans wore tuxedos to Miami's debut game on November 5, 1988, against the Los Angeles Clippers.

James Worthy was one of the All-Stars who were part of the league's midseason showcase game in Miami in 1990.

WELCOME, NBA

THE ALL-STAR GAME GETS SENT TO MIAMI

THIS WOULD be a solid trivia question: How many games did the Miami Heat win before the team was awarded the right to host an All-Star Game?

The answer is zero.

The Heat were off to an 0–14 start in year one when the NBA sent word that Miami would be the site of the league's All-Star weekend in February 1990, meaning all the best players in the world—Michael Jordan, Magic Johnson, Larry Bird, and many more—would be coming to South Florida.

Craig Hodges won the three-point shootout and Dominique Wilkins took home the dunk title at at All-Star Saturday that year in Miami. Cazzie Russell made the winning shot as the West beat the East 37–36 in the Legends Game.

And then Sunday, the main event. Miami Arena was spruced up, with video replay screens added at either end of the court for the first time. Johnson was the MVP with a game-high 22 points in a losing effort, as the East topped the West 130–113.

Miami pulled out all the stops; there were dinners, there was nightlife, there were even reports of a few players hitting golf courses over the weekend, something that can't happen during February in many NBA cities.

"This weekend was perfect," Johnson told reporters when it all was over. "I really liked coming to Miami. The city of Miami, the weather, they've been fantastic. I've really enjoyed myself this All-Star Game, more than any other city."

It would be the final playing appearance for Bird in an All-Star Game. He was picked for two others, but didn't compete in either.

1988
DECEMBER 14

THE FIRST WIN

HEAT 89, CLIPPERS 88

THE FIRST 17 games did not go well for the expansion Heat, to put it mildly.

They lost all 17. They gave up 138 points in a 47-point loss to Pat Riley and the Los Angeles Lakers in their eighth game, three games after managing only 65 points in a 19-point loss to the Boston Celtics. Of the 17 losses, 11 were by double figures but the others were close—a six-point loss in overtime, another six-point loss in regulation, a pair of four-point losses, a three-point defeat, and a two-point loss.

It was time for a breakthrough.

And it came on December 14, 1988, when the Heat met the Clippers—their opening-night opponent—once again. The Heat were up by nine at the half, pushed that lead to 10 points entering the fourth, and held on at the end for an 89–88 victory.

The first win.

Norm Nixon had a shot to win it as time was expiring for the Clippers, but his jumper from the right wing bounced off the rim. Coach Ron Rothstein threw his hands in the air in celebration, then wrapped his arms around Heat forward Pat Cummings and anyone else who came his way before he left the floor.

Cummings had 15 points for the Heat, as did Grant Long and Billy Thompson. The 17-game slide remains the longest losing streak in Heat history and the longest streak by an expansion team opening its first season.

But it was over. Finally.

Billy Thompson played with the Heat for their first three seasons and had 15 points in the franchise's first-ever win.

Rory Sparrow spent two seasons with the Heat, missing a total of two games in that span.

1989
FEBRUARY 17

RORY SPARROW
KING OF THE HEAT FIRSTS

RORY SPARROW had a slew of firsts in Miami Heat history. He had the first Heat basket in the franchise's inaugural game, a 14-foot jumper from the right side of the key against the Los Angeles Clippers on November 5, 1988. He had the first triple-double in team history as well, 24 points, 10 rebounds and 10 assists on April 18, 1989, against Dallas.

And on February 17, 1989, he had the first real buzzer-beater to win a game.

It came against the Charlotte Hornets. Sparrow got the ball with a few seconds left and Miami down by one. He tried going right but didn't see much of a pathway there, so he stopped and spun back into the lane. The shot came from about two feet inside the foul line, very near the spot where he had made that first Heat field goal a few months earlier.

Swish. Heat win, 103–102.

THE FIRST SEASON ENDS

15 WINS, 67 LOSSES

IT WAS not a banner first season for the Miami Heat. As expected, the expansion team struggled mightily. It finished with a 15–67 record, the worst in the NBA that season, and Miami was the only team in the league that didn't finish the season with a scoring average of at least 100 points per game.

But the ending is what coach Ron Rothstein would remember. The Heat won their finale, on the road, over playoff-bound Houston 91–89—escaping when Sleepy Floyd's three-point shot missed at the buzzer.

Miami had successfully rallied from a 15-point halftime deficit.

"It typifies our attitude all year long," Rothstein said after the game. "We never gave up. . . . To come up with this win tonight, I feel like we've won the NBA championship."

Kevin Edwards led that first Heat team in scoring with 13.8 points per game. He was followed by Rory Sparrow (12.5), Grant Long (11.9), Rony Seikaly (10.9), Billy Thompson (10.8), and Jon Sundvold (10.4).

There were a lot of rough nights in that first season. The Heat were outscored by 11.2 points per game, worst in the NBA that year. They won only three games by double figures (oddly, all of them by at least 20 points) and lost by 10 or more points 39 times. They lost five times by 32 points or more; Pat Riley and the Los Angeles Lakers were responsible for three of those blowouts.

But the framework was set, the foundation installed. Playoffs were still a long way off, but the Heat were ready to keep taking steps forward.

Houston's Sleepy Floyd missed a shot that would have beaten the Heat in their 1988–89 finale. The Heat won 91–89 and finished year one at 15–67.

Billy Thompson of the Heat defends in a game at Madison Square Garden against the New York Knicks.

THE SECOND SEASON BEGINS—BETTER, BUT A LONG WAY TO GO

YEAR TWO of the Heat brought a few more wins (three, to be exact). But it also brought hope.

The 18–64 record in 1989–90 was nothing to get excited about. The Heat still hadn't spent a day with a winning record and never had a winning streak in that second season longer than two games. The playoffs were quite obviously a long way off, even with a bit of improvement on the offensive end over the team's inaugural season.

Here's what they had: the league's most improved player in center Rony Seikaly and a pair of all-rookie selections—a first-teamer in guard Sherman Douglas (Seikaly's former Syracuse teammate), and a second-teamer in forward Glen Rice.

Those awards showed that the Heat were using the draft wisely. Rice, out of Michigan, was the fourth pick in the 1989 draft and Douglas was taken 28th overall by Miami.

The season went awry when the Heat dropped 23 out of 26 games during a two-month stretch from mid-November through mid-January. Seikaly averaged 16.6 points and 10.4 rebounds per game, Douglas averaged 14.3 points and 7.6 assists, and Rice averaged 13.6 points.

It was the start of the Sunshine State rivalry, with Orlando entering the NBA during the 1989–90 season. The Magic won the first-ever meeting between the teams; Miami won the next three that season to take the season series.

And the fan base continued to solidify, with the Heat announcing a sellout crowd of 15,008 for 40 of its 41 home games.

RONY SEIKALY HAS FIRST 40-POINT GAME IN HEAT HISTORY

IT WAS in a loss, so it wasn't a game that Rony Seikaly felt like celebrating. But on February 13, 1990, the Miami Heat center out of Syracuse grabbed a piece of Heat history.

He made 15 of 23 shots from the field along with 10 of 15 shots from the foul line against Michael Jordan and the Chicago Bulls and scored 40 points in a 107–95 loss at home. The significance: It was the first 40-point game in Heat history.

And it wasn't just the scoring. Seikaly also grabbed 17 rebounds in that game. It took 32 years before another Heat player—it just so happened to be LeBron James—finished a game with at least 40 points and 17 rebounds. (James had 40 points and 18 rebounds in a playoff win at Indiana on May 20, 2012, the Heat prevailing 101–93 in that contest.)

The 40-point game against Chicago was the only 40-point outing of Seikaly's career, counting his time with Miami and his three other NBA clubs—Orlando, Golden State, and New Jersey. There have been more than 80 such 40-point games in Heat franchise history since, but Seikaly's will forever be the first.

That night was also one of Seikaly's 221 double-doubles as a Heat player, a record that stood until Bam Adebayo passed him for the franchise lead in 2025.

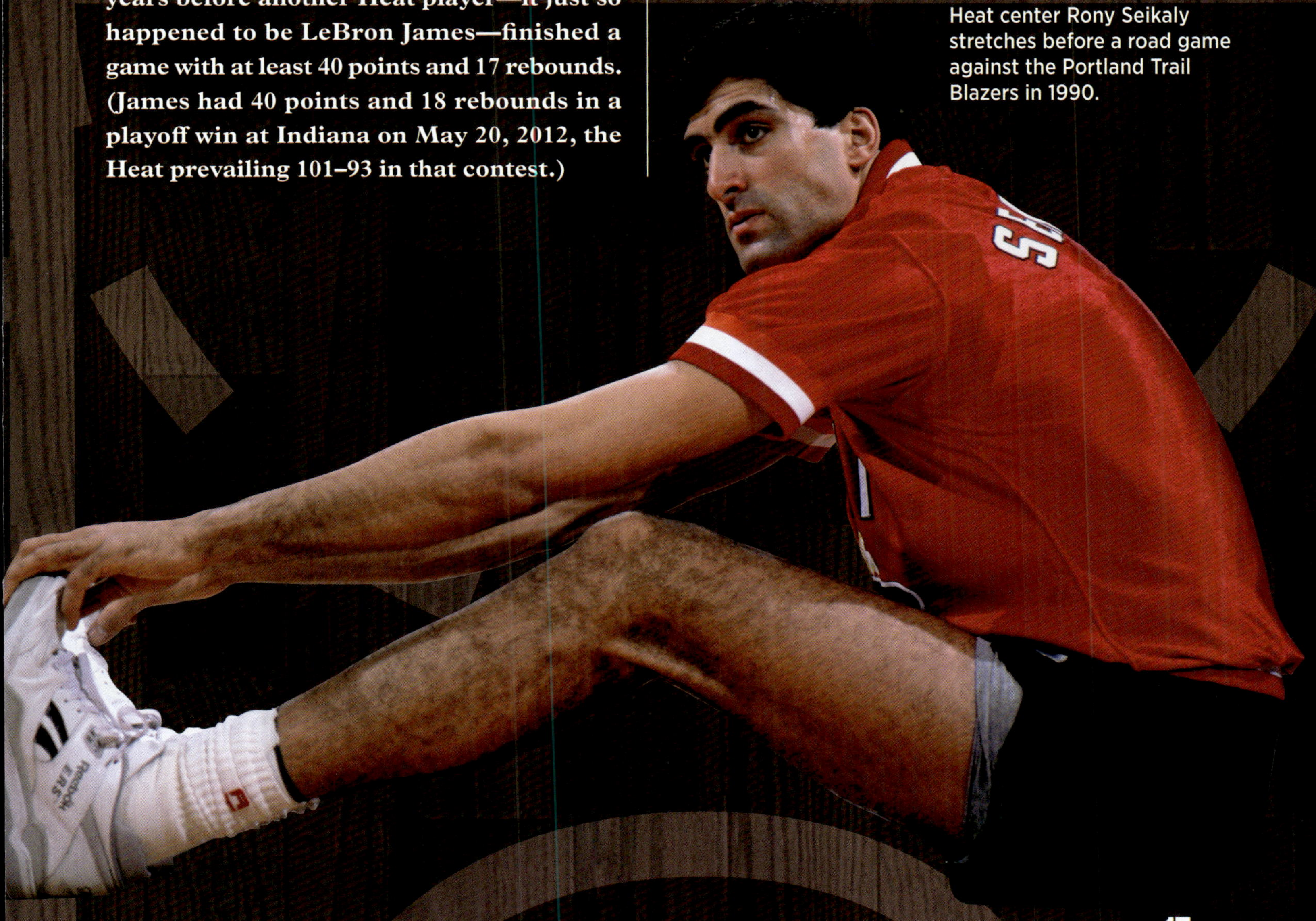

Heat center Rony Seikaly stretches before a road game against the Portland Trail Blazers in 1990.

SEIKALY WINS MOST IMPROVED PLAYER

THE MIAMI Heat showed serious improvement in the 1989–90 season, their second year in the NBA.

So, too, did Rony Seikaly.

The Heat center was the NBA's Most Improved Player for 1989–90, getting 37 out of 92 votes for the award and edging out sharpshooting guard Reggie Miller of the Indiana Pacers for the trophy.

Miller got 30 votes.

Seikaly, the former Syracuse University center, finished year two with the Heat averaging 16.6 points, 10.4 rebounds, and 1.7 blocked shots per game on 50 percent shooting.

Those were all major leaps over his year one numbers: 10.9 points, 7.0 rebounds and 1.2 blocks on 45 percent shooting.

But it's not like Seikaly—who didn't really have anyone to mentor him in those early Miami years—was content with the Most Improved Player trophy. On the day he learned that he won it, he announced plans to try to win it again the following season.

"I have a lot more that I can do," Seikaly said that day.

That plan didn't come to fruition, but Seikaly did increase his rebound-per-game numbers in each of the next two seasons and went on to average at least 17 points in a season twice.

Heat center Rony Seikaly dunks in a game at Portland in 1990.

1990
NOVEMBER 2

SEASON THREE BEGINS WITH A WIN

MARK THIS day down as one to remember: November 2, 1990.

The significance was this: Miami won a season-opener for the first time, and had a record over the .500 mark for the first time as well.

The third season of Heat basketball started with plenty of promise. Miami beat Washington 119–95 on opening night, getting 25 points from Willie Burton off the bench. It sparked a 3–3 start to the season by the Heat, by far the best of their three seasons.

The era of good fortune didn't last for long, as the Heat lost 16 of their next 18 games on the way to a 24–58 record. But it was a better record than years one and two, and the Heat matched a franchise-best with a three-game winning streak.

It was the same trio leading the way again for Miami, with Sherman Douglas averaging 18.5 points and 8.5 assists, Glen Rice averaging 17.4 points, and Rony Seikaly finishing the year averaging 16.4 points and 11.1 rebounds.

After the season, it was time for a big change. Coach Ron Rothstein, who went 57–189 in the first three seasons of Heat basketball, resigned in early May. Rothstein, who had been offered a chance to return even though his original three-year contract was up, cited the emotional toll on himself, his friends, and his family. "I decided I was not going to put myself through it anymore," Rothstein said.

So, for the first time since their infancy, the Heat were about to embark on a coaching search.

Sherman Douglas averaged 18.5 points and 8.5 assists in the 1990–91 season for the Heat.

1991
JUNE 17

KEVIN LOUGHERY
TAKES OVER AS HEAT COACH

THE MIAMI Heat didn't exist in 1971. They weren't even an idea in 1971. Kevin Loughery was still an NBA player in 1971.

But it turns out, that was the year when Loughery—unbeknownst to everyone—started the process of interviewing to become coach of the Heat.

Loughery spent the 1971–72 season with the Philadelphia 76ers and was teammates with Billy Cunningham that year. Cunningham was impressed with the way Loughery played and understood the game.

Fast forward two decades or so: Cunningham was part of the ownership group in Miami that was searching for the next Heat coach. And Loughery wound up being the pick, the person hired to take over for Ron Rothstein entering the fourth season of Heat basketball.

"I know he's the guy," Cunningham said. "He's someone who understands how to work with young players."

Loughery was accomplished. He had coached the New York Nets to a pair of ABA titles, those championship squads led by Julius Erving. He'd been an NBA coach in Atlanta, Washington, and Chicago, most notably serving as Michael Jordan's first coach with the Bulls.

He had the reputation of being a player's coach, and even Jordan said he enjoyed playing for him. Miami had improved on its win total in each of its first three seasons, and it was up to Loughery to get the Heat to the next level—that being playoff contention.

"I wanted one more opportunity," Loughery said. "I wanted to be where it mattered."

In Miami, he quickly learned that the Heat mattered.

1991
DECEMBER 17

OUCH! A RECORD-SETTING 68-POINT LOSS IN CLEVELAND

IT WASN'T that bad, at first. The Miami Heat were playing in Cleveland against the Cavaliers on December 17, 1991, and they found themselves trailing by only 10 points after the first quarter.

It was about to get worse. Much worse.

They were down 20 at halftime, down by 28 early in the third quarter when Kevin Lougherty pulled his starters, and kept them out for the remainder of the game, and then the floodgates really opened. Your final score: Cleveland 148, Miami 80, the worst loss at that point by any team in any game in NBA history.

"I don't know what we played," Heat star Glen Rice said that night, "but it wasn't basketball."

Before that night, the NBA record for biggest margin of victory had been untouched for nearly 20 years. The Los Angeles Lakers beat Golden State 162–99, a 63-point win, on March 19, 1972.

Miami's 68-point loss remained the widest margin of defeat in NBA history for nearly 30 years. Memphis beat Oklahoma City by 73 points—152–79—on December 2, 2021 to finally knock the Heat loss out of the top spot.

1992

APRIL 11

GLEN RICE BREAKS SHERMAN DOUGLAS'S SCORING RECORD

GLEN RICE was a scorer, plain and simple. It wasn't all he was, of course, but his biggest gift as a basketball player was the ability to shoot the ball from just about any place he wanted.

On April 11, 1992, with the Miami Heat fighting for a playoff spot, he went up against the Orlando Magic and put on an absolute show before the home fans.

He rewrote the Heat record book that night with 46 points, lifting Miami to a 105–101 victory over its in-state rival and moving the team a bit closer to its first-ever playoff spot. (Spoiler alert: The Heat would indeed qualify for those 1992 NBA playoffs, in just their fourth year in the league.)

Rice made 19 of his 32 field-goal attempts that night. He scored 31 points in the second half, including 16 points in the fourth quarter. The point total, his field-goal total, his field-goal attempt total, his second-half points, and his fourth-quarter points were all Heat records at that time.

The 46 points were four more than the previous Heat mark of 42, set by Sherman Douglas.

"I don't remember wanting the ball in any game as much as I did in that game that night," Rice would say years later. "It was a big moment. It was a big game for us. And I think I knew what it meant."

Glen Rice scored 46 points, then a franchse record, in a game for the Heat during the 1991–92 season.

THE HEAT MAKE THE PLAYOFFS FOR THE FIRST TIME

TALK ABOUT immediate impact.

In Kevin Loughery's first three weeks on the job as coach of the Heat in the 1991–92 season, the team had the longest winning streak in franchise history to that point—four games—and was off to a flying start. They were 6–2, by far the best record in Heat history.

After Miami beat Utah by 20 for that sixth win in the season's first eight games, Jazz point guard John Stockton offered a blunt assessment of the Heat. "They're good," he said, in what was likely one of the first instances of those two words being offered in consecutive order about a Heat team.

There were ups and there were downs, but entering the final days of the season Miami was in the playoff hunt.

And on the last day, April 19, 1992, Miami could have clinched a berth by beating Boston. It didn't happen; the Celtics topped the Heat 109–93. There was one chance left, but Cleveland had to beat Atlanta. The Cavaliers came through with a 112–108 win, and Miami had the last playoff spot in the Eastern Conference.

Their reward: a first-round series against Michael Jordan and the defending NBA champion Chicago Bulls.

"We'll probably sweep the Bulls," Loughery said, tongue clearly in cheek.

Well, he was half right. It was a sweep. Chicago ousted Miami in three games, winning Games 1 and 2 in blowouts at home and then coming to South Florida for a 119–114 win—Michael Jordan had 56 points in the clincher—that ended the first-ever Heat playoff season.

Bulls guard B.J. Armstrong looks for space against the double-team of Heat defenders Glen Rice and Kevin Edwards.

1993
APRIL 8

BRIAN SHAW MAKES 10 THREE-POINTERS

THE THREE-POINT shot was nowhere near as prevalent in 1993 as it is in this era of NBA basketball. Not everybody shot them. It wasn't something that happened every time down the floor.

That makes what Brian Shaw did for the Miami Heat on April 8 of that year even more special.

He didn't take a single free throw in Miami's road win against the Milwaukee Bucks that night. He took one two-point shot in that game and made it.

And he scored 32 points—30 of them on three-pointers.

Shaw set a club record that night with 10 three-pointers. Even more impressively, through the end of the 2024–25 season, that achievement remains in the Heat record book.

It has been tied on four occasions: Tyler Herro made 10 three-pointers in a game twice, Mario Chalmers did it once, and Duncan Robinson did it once.

But entering the 2025–26 season, Shaw's mark still has not been topped—even in an era when threes are wild in the NBA.

THE LOUGHERY ERA

A PLAYOFF RUN AND MORE CHANGES

THE 1992–93 season was a step back for the Heat, who missed the playoffs. They returned to the postseason in 1993–94 after the first winning season in team history—a 42–40 record. They even won a playoff game for the first time, taking a 2–1 series lead over Atlanta before falling to the Hawks in five games in 1994.

On the court, things were looking up.

Off the court the drama was really starting to brew.

Lewis Schaffel and Billy Cunningham owned part of the Heat and they were trying to sell, with much speculation focused on Whit Hudson as the potential buyer. That was significant, because Hudson was the brother-in-law of Wayne Huizenga, who owned the then-Florida Marlins, Florida Panthers, and Miami Dolphins at various times in his life.

Hudson thought they had a deal. Ted Arison, the biggest reason why Miami was given an expansion franchise in the 1980s, had left South Florida and re-emigrated to Israel. His son Micky Arison was a minority limited partner in the Heat, which didn't give him much of a say in team matters.

Ultimately, Micky Arison decided to buy his father's team back. It was perhaps the biggest decision in Heat history.

1995
FEBRUARY 13

MICKY ARISON PUTS HIS FAMILY BACK IN CONTROL OF THE HEAT

AT THE end of the 2024–25 NBA season, the Miami Heat were generally believed to be valued at $4 billion or more. Some NBA teams were selling for more than $6 billion at that point.

Either way, it was just more proof—as if any were needed—that Micky Arison made the right decision to buy back the team that his father Ted Arison played a huge role in founding.

That purchase, believed to be around $68 million, gave the Arison family control of the Heat once again. It was finalized on February 13, 1995. Micky Arison began making big moves the next day, firing Heat coach Kevin Loughery, replacing him with assistant coach Alvin Gentry for the remainder of the season, and bringing on former Heat assistant coach Dave Wohl as executive vice president overseeing basketball.

Arison went to All-Star weekend in Phoenix to look for more help. Wohl and Arison had no intention of making Gentry the long-term coach, so names were floated around and many thought a highly successful coach at the University of Cincinnati, Bob Huggins, was going to be the pick.

Arison, it turned out, had other ideas. He had someone already in mind to run his basketball team.

A PHONE CALL FROM PAT RILEY

AS HARD as it may be to believe now, the first time Pat Riley and Micky Arison met did not go particularly well.

It was February 1995. Arison had recently assumed control of the franchise that his father essentially started. He spent the All-Star break that season in Phoenix and was meeting with representatives of potential coaches and others who might want to move to Miami and help turn the Heat into a consistent winner.

Pat Riley, then of the New York Knicks, poses while diagramming a play. Riley left for the Heat in 1995.

Arison and Riley did not meet in Phoenix. They were not on each other's radar screens at that moment. Riley—then the coach of the New York Knicks—was coming to Miami soon after the break anyway, since his team was visiting the Heat. And during that visit, with the Knicks going through their shootaround practice, someone asked Arison if he wanted to meet Riley.

Dave Wohl, then the Heat executive vice president of basketball operations, introduced them. Wohl knew Riley well since he was previously on his staff in Los Angeles, which allowed him to broker the meeting. Arison and Riley chatted for just a couple of minutes. Arison thought Riley was distracted. Riley was trying to get his team ready for a game.

"The last thing he wanted to do was meet me," Arison would say years later.

A couple months later, Arison got a phone call from someone who said he was representing Riley. Rumors were flying that Riley would consider leaving New York. Arison was presented with a list of terms that Riley would want if he ever left the Knicks.

Arison didn't shy away from the list. The talks continued. And then Arison, on his way to Key West from Miami one day, got a phone call.

"Hello," the caller said. "This is Pat Riley."

The Heat fortunes were about to change.

A DINNER IN BOSTON SHAPES HEAT HISTORY

PAT RILEY might have been coaching the New York Knicks in 1995, but at his core, he was still probably a Los Angeles Laker. And if you're a Laker, you don't like the Boston Celtics.

That fact made the next phase of the Miami Heat deciding whether Riley would be their next coach both ironic and hilarious. In the summer of 1995 Arison was staying on a yacht in New England. He wanted to meet with Riley, so plans were made for Riley and his wife Chris to fly up to Boston.

Boston. The mere mention of the word could get Riley going. Celtics–Lakers games were no joke in those days, so it was odd that Riley would be shaping his future by a meeting in that city.

The Rileys boarded the yacht and met Arison, his wife, and their children. They dined together before Riley and Arison retired to a private office to talk about the future. A handshake deal was struck. Riley told himself that he was the next coach of the Heat and knew the Knicks would be furious about it.

The Knicks learned of the meeting and claimed that the Heat had tampered with Riley since he was under contract with New York. Riley sent his resignation letter by fax, only further angering the

Heat coach Pat Riley and Managing General Partner Micky Arison talk during the 2006 NBA Finals in Miami.

IMAGINATION

Knicks. The NBA had to get involved. Riley was worried. The Heat were in trouble.

Finally, on September 1, 1995, everyone agreed on a deal. The Knicks got $1 million and a draft pick. The Heat got Pat Riley. It was done.

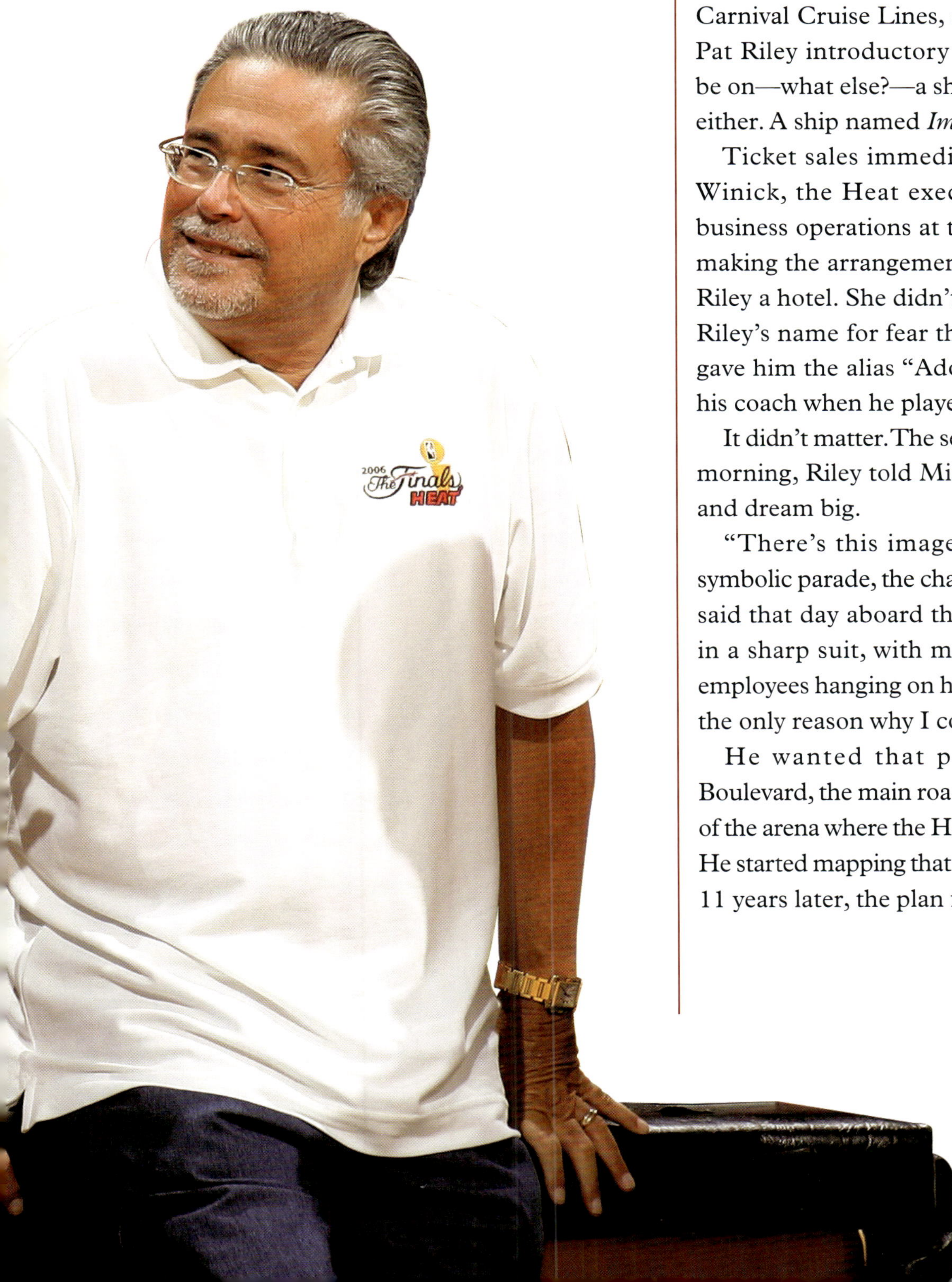

WHEN THE Miami Heat and Pat Riley could finally strike a deal, it was time for the new coach and team president to meet Miami.

What really happened was Miami wound up meeting Pat Riley.

Micky Arison and his family owned and operated Carnival Cruise Lines, so it made sense that the Pat Riley introductory press conference would be on—what else?—a ship. And not just any ship, either. A ship named *Imagination*.

Ticket sales immediately exploded. Pauline Winick, the Heat executive vice president of business operations at the time, was tasked with making the arrangements. It came time to book Riley a hotel. She didn't want to put the room in Riley's name for fear that he'd be found, so she gave him the alias "Adolph Rupp," the name of his coach when he played at Kentucky.

It didn't matter. The secret got out. And the next morning, Riley told Miami it was time to dream and dream big.

"There's this image in my mind about the symbolic parade, the championship parade," Riley said that day aboard the ship, dressed as always in a sharp suit, with media members and Heat employees hanging on his every word. "And that's the only reason why I coach."

He wanted that parade down Biscayne Boulevard, the main road that runs along the front of the arena where the Heat play their home games. He started mapping that out in his mind, even. And 11 years later, the plan finally became a reality.

1995
APRIL 15

RICE SCORES 56 POINTS IN A HEAT WIN

THE ORLANDO Magic played a brilliant game on April 15, 1995.

Shaquille O'Neal had 38 points and 16 rebounds. Anfernee Hardaway scored 28 points. Horace Grant and Nick Anderson combined for 41 more points. The Magic's best players were rolling that night.

They were no match for Glen Rice.

He could not miss: 20 for 27 from the field, seven for eight from three-point range, nine for 10 from the foul line. Add it up, and it was a 56-point night—a Heat single-game record that stood for nearly two decades.

The Heat won the game, 123–117. They were down six going into the fourth quarter, then outscored the Magic 36–24 in the final 12 minutes.

Glen Rice had a year to remember in 1995 for the Miami Heat, winning the three-point contest at All-Star weekend and setting a team record with a 56-point game.

MIAMI

Heat coach Pat Riley talks to his team during his first season with the club, 1995–96.

RILEY TAKES OVER

THE FALL of 1995 was like none other for the Miami Heat.

Pat Riley had taken over as president and head coach of the Heat, Micky Arison had taken over as managing general partner a few months earlier, and Miami was looking to become a championship organization.

There were growing pains. There was growing to do.

Riley didn't have an office for the first few weeks; he was working out of a conference room and doing a lot of travel around the country. Riley had scheduled a slew of speaking engagements because he thought the NBA was going to suspend him because he had talked with the Heat while under contract with the New York Knicks.

Those flights gave Riley time to think, time to plan, and time to build a new Miami staff.

It all had to happen quickly. Riley decided to bring in Randy Pfund as executive vice president of player personnel, in part because the two men had worked together before and understood one another. Shortly after the Pfund move, Riley hired Scotty Robertson, Bob McAdoo, and Stan Van Gundy as assistant coaches, landed Jeff Bzdelik as assistant coach and scout and offered the same role—assistant and scout—to Tony Fiorentino, who had been with the Heat since the beginning.

Other front-office moves were happening, and Riley began the process of putting his stamp on every element of the organization: how the team dressed, how it traveled, how it worked. No detail was too small for Riley in the early days.

The biggest moves, however, were yet to come. There was a roster to transform. There was a splash to make.

1995

NOVEMBER 3

ALONZO MOURNING COMES TO MIAMI

GLEN RICE was a fan favorite in Miami, had just won the three-point contest at All-Star weekend, barely missed a game in his first six seasons with the Heat, averaged at least 21 points in three of those six years, and had more than lived up to the billing he came in with as the No. 4 pick in the 1989 draft.

Pat Riley arrived in Miami thinking Rice would be a cornerstone, someone to build a winner around.

But Riley also believed that dominant centers were vital. He had coached Kareem Abdul-Jabbar with the Los Angeles Lakers. He had coached Patrick Ewing with the New York Knicks. That's why, one day before his debut with the Heat, the team pulled off a blockbuster deal: Rice was going to Charlotte and Alonzo Mourning was coming to Miami.

"I came here," Mourning would say, "because of coach Riley."

The full deal was Rice, Matt Geiger, Khalid Reeves, and a first-round draft pick (one that became Tony Delk in 1996) to the Hornets for Mourning, LeRon Ellis, and Pete Myers.

It was a significant price, but a price that Riley felt was necessary to pay. A night later, he and Mourning made their Miami debuts. Mourning scored 15 points and the Heat held Cleveland to 24 points in the second half on the way to a blue-collar, grind-it-out 85–71 win over the Cavaliers.

Riley wrote "ALIVE" on the board in the team's locker room before the game. The Heat were alive. The Riley era was alive. A new plan in Miami was taking shape.

Miami acquired Voshon Lenard later in that 1995–96 season and traded for Tim Hardaway in February 1996. The Heat always tended to be conservative before Riley came along. No more. They were swinging for the fences.

Alonzo Mourning, shown dunking, was the first big name the Heat acquired during the Pat Riley era.

JALOPY 1 AND JALOPY 2

IT'S A story that Pat Riley has told for decades. He says one of the first conversations he had with Managing General Partner Micky Arison after Riley got to take over as coach and president of the Miami Heat involved a simple question from the man who was becoming his new boss.

"Do you know how much it costs to win a championship?" Arison asked, by Riley's recollection.

The answer: "I'll tell you when we win one."

Riley came to the Heat and wanted to change everything. That didn't just mean on the court. He changed the way the Heat warmed up for games. He wanted to add a family room, which still exists today and is the pregame or in-game meeting spot for players, staff, and their guests. Anything that Riley thought was gimmicky was tuned down or eliminated entirely.

And then there were the planes.

Only a few people within the organization are still there from those days, but they remember—note, we did not say "fondly" remember—the way the Heat used to travel to games. There were two planes that the Heat used in the early days of flying charter; they were called Jalopy 1 and Jalopy 2.

Riley wasn't going to stand for that.

He wanted Arison and the Heat to buy a plane. The initial answer was no. So, Riley bluffed and said he would buy the plane himself. Arison knew he was bluffing but approved a plane upgrade anyway.

It was just one of the many ways that the Heat were set to fly in the Riley era.

Pat Riley and the Miami Heat land back at Miami International Airport, returning from Dallas after winning the 2006 NBA Finals.

MOURNING SCORES 50

IT MIGHT have been the best game of Alonzo Mourning's career.

He had 21 points in the first quarter alone on his way to finishing with a career-best 50 for the Miami Heat in their 112–93 win on March 29, 1996 over the Washington Bullets.

Mourning was 17 of 24 from the floor and 16 of 17 from the foul line, and he added 12 rebounds. His big night came two nights after a game Miami lost to the Los Angeles Lakers by nine points, and Mourning blamed himself for that defeat.

"I had extra incentive," he said after the 50-point game.

The Heat were in no way surprised by how Mourning bounced back.

"He was tortured for 48 hours by what happened the other night," Heat coach Pat Riley told reporters after that game. "He came back strong and with a vengeance."

Alonzo Mourning battles for two of his 50 points in a game against Washington on March 29, 1996.

P.J. Brown of the Heat and Charles Oakley of the Knicks battle for a loose ball during a Miami-New York game. At that time, the rivalry was one of the NBA's fiercest.

HEAT-KNICKS
THE RIVALRY TAKES OFF

IN THE 1997 NBA Eastern Conference semifinals, the Miami Heat trailed the New York Knicks 3–1 in the series.

"We had to show some fight," Heat coach Pat Riley said.

His words might have been taken a bit too literally, and a rivalry was set to absolutely explode on the NBA's playoff stage.

The Knicks and Heat already hated each other. Riley quit coaching the Knicks after the 1994–95 season—by sending a fax—with a year left on his contract. The Heat eventually got Riley out of his Knicks contract for $1 million and a first-round draft pick, and the New York–Miami rivalry in basketball was born.

And it only got hotter.

That East semifinal series changed when New York's Charlie Ward and Miami's P.J. Brown got tangled under the basket during Game 5, a matchup to which both sides were bringing a level of physicality and were complaining to referees after just about every call. Ward got flipped over, tempers were flaring, tension was rising, the fans were vocal about how they wanted more, and four Knicks—Allan Houston, Patrick Ewing, Larry Johnson and John Starks—all were suspended for leaving the Knicks' bench to join the fight.

Ward and Brown were suspended, as were Houston, Ewing, Johnson, and Starks. Johnson and Starks had to miss Game 7 of that series; the other Knicks missed Game 6, and Brown missed both remaining games of the series for Miami.

The Heat staved off all three elimination chances, winning the series 4–3.

ISAAC AUSTIN WINS MOST IMPROVED PLAYER

THERE WERE a slew of good candidates for the Most Improved Player award for the 1996–97 season. Toronto's Doug Christie was thought of as one, as was Portland's Rasheed Wallace.

And the Miami Heat had two legitimate hopefuls as well in Issac Austin and Voshon Lenard.

In the end, it was Austin's year.

His numbers weren't eye-popping: 9.7 points, 5.8 rebounds, and 1.2 assists per game on 50 percent shooting while only playing about 23 minutes per contest.

But he played a valuable role off the bench for a Pat Riley–coached team that won 61 games, and voters took notice.

He also had a compelling story. Austin was a second-round pick in 1991, only averaged 1.1 points per game as a rookie in Utah, then lasted two more NBA seasons before heading to France and Turkey for two years in an effort to revive his career.

The Heat brought him back to the NBA in 1996, and his improvement was clearly noticed.

Isaac Austin (center) celebrates a playoff win with Heat teammates Voshon Lenard (left) and Dan Majerle (right).

Chris Childs (left) and John Starks of the Knicks battle Heat guard Tim Hardaway during Game 5 of Round 1 of the 1998 playoffs.

HEAT–KNICKS AGAIN

A LEG GRAB AND A FRIENDLY ROLL

THE MIAMI Heat and New York Knicks met again in the 1998 playoffs, the second of four consecutive years of postseason matchups between the rival franchises.

The Heat were favored in the best-of-five first-round series, but split the first two games at home and had to win at least one in New York to have a chance in the series. The Heat got that needed win in Game 3 and had a chance to close the Knicks out in Game 4 at Madison Square Garden.

It was a fight. More accurately, there were fights.

It was a game probably best remembered for a fight between Alonzo Mourning and Larry Johnson—and the image of New York coach Jeff Van Gundy, down on the ground, trying to pull Mourning away by grabbing onto his leg.

It was a mess. Patrick Ewing was suspended for Game 5, as were Mourning and Johnson. The NBA kept Johnson out of the deciding Heat-Knicks game for the second straight year.

Allan Houston scored 30 points, and the Knicks eased past Miami 98–81 to win the series 3–2. Miami never led that game and spent much of it trailing by double digits, before Tim Hardaway's three-pointer with about 7:10 left got the Heat within two points at 72–70.

The Knicks closed the game on a 26–11 run to win the series—and went on to eliminate Miami in 1999 and 2000 as well.

MOURNING WINS DEFENSIVE PLAYER OF THE YEAR

THE BELIEF going into awards-voting time after the labor strike–shortened 1998–99 season in the NBA was that defensive player of the year would come down to a pair of former Georgetown centers: Alonzo Mourning of the Miami Heat and Dikembe Mutombo of the Atlanta Hawks.

It was a one-sided result.

Mourning got 89 of a possible 118 votes and won the DPOY award that season, with Mutombo finishing a distant second and Seattle SuperSonics guard Gary Payton—who would eventually play for the Heat—finishing third.

Mutombo had the edge in rebounds per game over Mourning, 12.2 to 11.0. But Mourning blocked 3.9 shots per game that season, 1.0 more than Mutombo, and that likely was one of the things that swayed voters his way.

Heat center Alonzo Mourning, in his prime, was generally considered the NBA's best defensive player.

Miami's Jamal Mashburn fights for the ball against Orlando's Monty Williams in a game on January 2, 2000.

THE HEAT GET A NEW HOME AND A WIN

MIDWAY THROUGH the 1999–2000 season, the Miami Heat were on the move. Literally.

On January 2, 2000, the Heat moved into their new home—then called AmericanAirlines Arena. It is the same building they use in 2025, though the name has changed a few times over that quarter-century.

And it was christened in style, with a win. Miami beat the Orlando Magic 111–103 in overtime.

"It's a dream come true," Heat coach Pat Riley said that night. "It's a first-class facility for the fans, the players and the city to feel proud of. One day we'd really, really, really like to celebrate the ultimate win here."

Built at a cost of about $215 million, the 19,600-seat structure was state-of-the-art. And sitting courtside that night was Florida Governor Jeb Bush, who gave the place his official approval.

"It's fantastic," Bush said.

MOURNING WINS NBA DEFENSIVE PLAYER OF THE YEAR AGAIN

IN THE 1999–2000 season, nobody in the NBA was as dominant as Shaquille O'Neal of the Los Angeles Lakers. He finished with 29.7 points, 13.6 rebounds, 3.8 assists, and 3.0 blocks per game on his way to becoming the near-unanimous pick as the league's most valuable player.

But for as good as O'Neal was, the best defender in the league—for the second consecutive season—played for the Miami Heat.

Alonzo Mourning won the defensive player of the year award for the second consecutive season. The final voting numbers weren't as one-sided as they had been the previous year, but he still collected more than 50 percent of the votes cast—62 out of a possible 121. The key again was blocked shots; Mourning averaged 3.7 of those per game that season.

O'Neal finished second in the DPOY race, with future Heat guard Eddie Jones of the Charlotte Hornets and Dikembe Mutombo of the Atlanta Hawks tying for third.

Alonzo Mourning (right) receives the defensive player of the year award from NBA legend Bill Russell.

2000
OCTOBER

MOURNING GETS SICK

THERE WERE plenty of trials and tribulations in the early years of the Pat Riley era with the Miami Heat. They made the playoffs in each of his first six years, won the franchise's first-ever playoff series in 1997—two, in fact—and made their way to the East finals to face Michael Jordan and the Chicago Bulls.

And then came 1998, 1999, and 2000. The Knicks ruined those seasons.

Miami's 55-win season in 1997–98 ended in a first-round, best-of-five, Game 5, at-home loss to the Knicks. Miami had the No. 1 seed after finishing with a 33–17 record in the shortened 1998–99 season, again losing in five games to the Knicks when Allan Houston scored with less than a second left in the deciding game. In 2000, Miami and New York met again in the East semifinals; the Knicks won a Game 7. And all three of those season-ending losses to the Knicks came in Miami, two by exactly one point.

It got worse.

Alonzo Mourning helped the US win gold at the Sydney Olympics in 2000, shortly before he learned that he had a severe kidney disease called Focal Segmental Glomerulosclerosis. Mourning originally feared he wouldn't play again. He came back for the final 13 games of the following season.

"This was life-threatening," Mourning said. "You're dealing with a life-threatening situation, and my employers were deeply concerned about my health because they know all that I put out every night on the court."

The Heat missed the playoffs in 2002 and 2003. The franchise needed something good to happen. Mourning said "for every adversity there's a seed of equivalent benefit."

The adversity was losing. The benefit was the No. 5 pick in the 2003 draft. That became Dwyane Wade.

Alonzo Mourning at the October 2000 news conference when he discusses stepping away from the game because of illness.

MOURNING RETURNS

HE MISSED his first shot. And his second. And his third. And his fourth. And his fifth. Nobody minded. The story was bigger than any stat on March 27, 2001.

Alonzo Mourning was back in a Miami Heat uniform that day for the first time since being diagnosed with a serious kidney problem the previous fall. When his illness was made public, some wondered if his career was over. Turns out, his season wasn't even over.

Mourning returned with 13 games left in the 2000–01 Heat season. His first basket that night against the Toronto Raptors was—what else? —a dunk. He finished 3 for 11 from the field and scored nine points in Miami's 101–92 loss.

Nobody was happy about the result. Everybody was thrilled about the return.

"Let's get away from Alonzo Mourning the patient," he said that night, "and start talking about Alonzo Mourning the basketball player."

Alonzo Mourning returned from a serious kidney issue and finished the 2000–01 season, defying long odds along the way.

Dwyane Wade poses after being selected by Miami in the 2003 NBA draft.

HOW THE HEAT DRAFT MINDS WORKED

IF DWYANE Wade recalls correctly, he worked out for about two-thirds of the NBA teams going into the 2003 draft.

His worst workout—according to Wade himself—was with the Miami Heat.

The Heat had the No. 5 pick in the draft that year and were linked to several different players. Pat Riley always likes power forwards and centers, so Chris Kaman was a logical choice for the Heat list. So was Chris Bosh, the super-smooth freshman out of Georgia Tech. Texas guard T.J. Ford was highly thought of as well.

But Riley liked Wade, which is odd, because he initially disliked Wade—sort of. We'll explain.

Riley went to Kentucky and starred there for Adolph Rupp in the 1960s. Wade and his Marquette team played Kentucky in the 2003 NCAA Tournament. (Riley watched some of it while on a treadmill in a hotel.) Wade had a triple-double in that game to beat Kentucky. Riley hated the outcome, but found himself really liking Wade.

"I always knew that I was going to draft Dwyane or Chris Bosh, whoever was there," Riley would say years later.

Wade was nervous for the Heat workout. Riley tried to calm him down by shaking his hand. It was the handshake—the way Wade responded, the size of his hand, the strength, all of it—that convinced Riley once and for all who the Heat had to draft.

"There wasn't anybody who talked me out of anything," Riley said. "Dwyane Wade was the guy."

DWYANE AND UDONIS

A MATCH MADE IN HEAT HEAVEN

WHEN THE Miami Heat drafted Dwyane Wade, there was one person who was not immediately impressed.

Turns out, Udonis Haslem had never seen the person who would soon become his teammate, one of his best friends, someone he would eventually call a brother, play.

"One of my best friends told me, 'Y'all got the steal of the draft. Dwyane Wade from Marquette,'" Haslem once said.

Haslem was puzzled. "I was like, 'Who is that?'" he said.

He was about to find out.

When Wade got to South Florida, he knew who Haslem was—sort of, anyway. More on that in a moment. Wade remembered seeing Haslem play at Florida; Haslem's college days with the Gators ended a year before Wade's did at Marquette.

As the story goes, they were in the Heat practice facility together in the summer of 2003 before the NBA summer league was starting. Wade noticed a rather aggressive individual getting most of the rebounds. He asked someone who it was.

"That's Udonis Haslem," he was told.

Wade was in disbelief. "No, it's not," he said.

But it was Haslem—a very, very slimmed-down Haslem from what Wade remembered in college. (Haslem spent a year playing in France and lost a ton of weight, transforming his body into a frame that could play in the NBA.)

Haslem is from Miami. Wade isn't. But they became fast friends. That first summer, they were inseparable: lived in the same hotel, did track workouts in the morning at the University of Miami, then headed to the arena, did workouts, had lunch, played pickup games, and repeated the process the next day.

"You can't not build a relationship or a bond with a person when you go through that," Haslem said.

Dwyane Wade and Udonis Haslem became Heat legends, playing for the franchise's first three title-winning teams.

Pat Riley (right) speaks at a 2003 news conference announcing that Stan Van Gundy (left) would take over as coach. Heat Managing General Partner Micky Arison looks on.

"ARE YOU READY?"

THE START of the 2003–04 Miami Heat season was six days away. Dwyane Wade would be going into his rookie season, as would Miami native Udonis Haslem. There was optimism in the air. The Heat had reason to believe.

And then on that one morning, early on a Wednesday, Heat coach Pat Riley knocked on assistant coach Stan Van Gundy's door.

"Are you ready?"

That was the question. The answer was irrelevant. Riley already knew what was going to happen.

He formally announced two days later that he was stepping down as coach. Van Gundy was taking over.

"I just believe that with this new team and these guys and the flexibility that we have that another voice is needed on the court," Riley said at a news conference that came out of nowhere. "I'm firmly convinced about that. And I think it's Stan's voice. That's why I did this."

Turns out, Riley had suggested this to Van Gundy two or three times during the previous 18 months. He'd hint that he was turning the team over. Van Gundy would wait for him to inevitably change his mind the next day. Only this time, the next day didn't bring any change of heart.

It was real. Stan Van Gundy was the new coach of the Heat. He had been a college head coach before, three years at what was then called Castleton State (now Castleton University) in Vermont, four years at UMass-Lowell, one year at Wisconsin.

And now, this.

"I'm not going to try to be Pat Riley," Van Gundy said. "I don't think it's a difference in philosophy so much as we're just different people. I'm not getting into those comparisons. I'm certainly not looking to make a lot of Pat Riley comparisons here to begin with."

Was he ready? The Heat were about to find out.

OH, BROTHER
STAN VAN GUNDY VS. JEFF VAN GUNDY

THE SEVENTH game of the 2003–04 Miami Heat season had some special significance, and not because the Heat were about to fall to 0–7 in Dwyane Wade's rookie year.

It was a brother vs. brother coaching matchup.

Stan Van Gundy was coaching the Heat, and Jeff Van Gundy was coaching the Houston Rockets. The Rockets won 90–70, and the Van Gundys joined Herb Brown and Larry Brown as the only brothers to face off as opposing coaches in an NBA game.

Stan Van Gundy spent the evening before the game at his brother's Houston home. Steak, potatoes, salad, and tons of basketball talk were on the menu.

"It's never a distraction when you can see your brother," Jeff Van Gundy told reporters before the game. "We sat around saying things like 'your team is better,' and the other saying, 'no, your team is better.' We wasted a lot of time doing that."

For the record, Stan and the Heat won the rematch on January 26, 2004, 95–81 behind 27 from Eddie Jones and a 20-point, 15-rebound night from Lamar Odom.

The brothers would go head-to-head five times in all. Home court was the difference, evidently; Stan Van Gundy went 3–0 against his brother when the games were in Miami, and Jeff Van Gundy went 2–0 against his brother when the games were in Houston.

Jeff Van Gundy (standing) and Stan Van Gundy (seated) would coach against one another in five Rockets–Heat games.

Heat guard Dwyane Wade rises to score over Baron Davis of New Orleans in the final moments of Game 1 of the 2004 NBA playoffs in Miami.

WADE'S FIRST PLAYOFF GAME

AND FIRST PLAYOFF HEROICS

IT WAS Dwyane Wade's first playoff game: Game 1, Round 1, at home against New Orleans to open the 2004 postseason. The Miami Heat had blown a 12-point lead in about seven minutes of the fourth quarter, and the game was tied at 79 with 11 seconds left.

He did not know who was taking the last shot.

Luckily for him, Heat coach Stan Van Gundy did.

"He's there drawing it up, I'm seeing it happen and I realize that he's doing this for me," Wade said years later.

NBA plays are fairly elaborate in some cases. There's the first option, the second option, a third option, and sometimes even more. Van Gundy went all-in with that play. There was no second option. The rookie was getting the ball and he was going to decide the game. That was it.

The ball comes in. Wade dribbles a few times, then takes a hard step and dribbles to the right to get Baron Davis moving away from him. Wade takes a 10-footer. He thought it might have been too far to the right. It wasn't. Heat lead, Heat get a stop to end the game, Heat win.

"I didn't know it," Wade said later, "but I was waiting for that shot my whole life."

The Heat would win the series, before bowing to Indiana in six games in Round 2. But for a team that started 0–7, it was generally considered an outstanding start to the Wade era. And the team was already thinking about who it could add to the mix before the next season.

A few months later, a tractor-trailer pulled up to the arena and Shaquille O'Neal hopped out of the cab. The Heat were about to become a serious title contender.

BEFORE TRADING SHAQUILLE O'NEAL TO MIAMI,

THE LAKERS HAD ANOTHER TRADE IN MIND

THE WORD was out. The Los Angeles Lakers were going to make big changes going into the 2004–05 season. And Miami Heat President Pat Riley never passed up opportunities.

Lakers owner Jerry Buss, Riley's old boss, wanted to have a talk. The Heat agreed to let it happen.

Buss had an idea: Come back to the Lakers, he told Riley. Wine flowed freely that night. Had it happened, it would have essentially been a deal where the Lakers would make a trade with the Heat for Riley.

Another trade was on Riley's mind. He wanted Shaquille O'Neal in Miami.

So, the talks pivoted. The Lakers asked for Dwyane Wade. The Heat instantly declined that one. Anyone else, sure, the Heat said. But not Wade. The deal became Caron Butler, Lamar Odom, Brian Grant, and a first-round draft pick for O'Neal.

Everything was about to change for Miami. And Riley stayed put to see it all happen.

Shaquille O'Neal poses at his introductory news conference as a member of the Miami Heat in 2004.

THE SUMMER OF SHAQ

A SUMMER OF CHANGE

THE TRADE for Shaquille O'Neal sent shock waves through the NBA . . . and the Miami Heat organization, for that matter.

It led Dwyane Wade to wonder how that Round 1 win over New Orleans might have set the franchise up for everything that would happen over the next decade.

"If one moment goes differently, you have to wonder what else changes," Wade said.

That was in response to a question about his first playoff game and his first playoff game-winning shot, one that beat New Orleans in Round 1, Game 1 of the 2004 playoffs. That shot helped the Heat go on to win the series in seven games. That playoff win might have been the reason why the Heat decided to trade for O'Neal. Landing O'Neal helped Miami win the 2006 NBA title. That led to the start of planning for the next Heat core and what might happen in the ballyhooed free-agent summer of 2010. That led to Wade staying and Chris Bosh and LeBron James coming to the Heat. And that led to four consecutive NBA Finals appearances and two more championships in that span.

"Some of it might have happened. All of it might have happened. None of it might have happened," Wade said. "We'll never know. Thank God we'll never know."

Heat fans celebrated the arrival of Shaquille O'Neal outside the team's arena in 2004.

Shaquille O'Neal lifts the key to Miami-Dade County, presented to him by County Mayor Alex Penelas (center) in 2004.

HOW "FLASH" WAS BORN

SHAQUILLE O'NEAL knew plenty about what NBA dynamic duos are like. He was with Kobe Bryant when they were Los Angeles Lakers teammates. Sometimes, it was great. Sometimes, not so much. It was no secret that they clashed. And it was obviously no secret that they won: the 2000, 2001 and 2002 NBA championships proved that.

In 2004, O'Neal was traded to the Miami Heat.

And one of O'Neal's first orders of official Heat business was getting to know Dwyane Wade.

O'Neal gave Wade the nickname "Flash." Wade didn't like it at first, but when O'Neal decides something, it's decided. O'Neal said Wade was flash-fast with a basketball in his hands, so Flash it was.

Shaq and Flash. It was catchy.

But for Shaq and Flash to work, Shaq had to tell Flash about Shaq and Kobe. All of it. The good and the bad. So, Wade and O'Neal went out to eat, long before anyone knew they'd even gotten together. O'Neal talked. Wade listened. And Wade learned.

"He told me that they were unstoppable, and how the only two people that could stop Shaq and Kobe were Shaq and Kobe," Wade said. "He promised me that wouldn't happen with us, that he was going to lift me to the places I needed to be and that he wouldn't get in my way."

Wade was only going into year two of his career. By year three, he was an NBA champion. O'Neal actually handed him the NBA Finals MVP trophy.

O'Neal delivered on every promise he made to Flash.

Dwyane Wade and Shaquille O'Neal pose before a game in the 2004–05 season.

WADE TRIES TO PLAY THROUGH PAIN,

BUT HEAT FALL SHORT OF MAKING NBA FINALS

SHAQUILLE O'NEAL and Dwyane Wade were one game away from getting to the NBA Finals together in their first season as Miami Heat teammates.

And in the end, that meant they were one game short.

Miami wasted a 3–2 lead in the Eastern Conference finals that season against the Detroit Pistons, losing in a rout at Auburn Hills, Michigan, in Game 6 and then falling 88–82 at home in Game 7.

Wade couldn't play in Game 6 because of a rib muscle injury. He played in Game 7 and scored 20 points, but he wasn't his usual self because of how limiting the injury was.

"I couldn't give my all-out effort that my teammates deserved and that Miami deserved," Wade said. "But I gave it as much as I could."

He lived in the training room to try and get ready for Game 7. He even took a painkilling injection in his chest in an effort to play.

Said Heat coach Stan Van Gundy: "When somebody is having to stick a needle in your chest just so you can go out and play . . . I thought he was phenomenal."

Year one of Shaq and Flash fell just short. Year two would go a bit better.

"We still had a lot of opportunities to win," O'Neal said. "I'm proud of the guys. They fought hard."

Shaquille O'Neal extends a hand to Dwyane Wade after the Heat guard got knocked to the floor during a game in 2005.

VAN GUNDY STEPS DOWN, *RILEY RETURNS*

THE MIAMI Heat were 21 games into the 2005–06 season. They were 11–10. Not great, not bad. Not good enough for anyone's liking.

Unknown to most people at the time, Stan Van Gundy had been having second thoughts about coaching. And third thoughts. And fourth. And . . . you get the idea.

Eventually, Heat Managing General Partner Micky Arison had no choice but to accept Van Gundy's resignation. Van Gundy wasn't happy and said coaching was making him regret the time that it would take away from his family.

Van Gundy had replaced Pat Riley in 2003. In 2005, it went the other way. Riley returned.

"I will get back into this quickly," said Riley, then a 60-year-old team president who was planning for a hip replacement surgery, not coaching.

Van Gundy, at a hastily called news conference, said he would have seen his kids for just 49 days out of the 170 days in the season.

"That's just not enough anymore for me. It's just not enough," Van Gundy said on that December 2005 day. "I mean, it's been like that for my kids' entire lives. I've got a 14-year-old daughter and it started to hit me when I started thinking about her birthday, which was last month. I've got four more years left with her. Four. And then she'll be off to college and I'm just not willing to sacrifice any more of those four more years."

Riley started to tear up as Van Gundy talked. He tried to persuade Van Gundy to stay. It didn't work.

Van Gundy left the Heat with a regular-season record of 112–73. He had been Riley's top assistant for eight seasons, getting promoted shortly before the 2003–04 campaign when Riley walked into his office unexpectedly and told him he was stepping aside.

That move stunned Heat fans. So did this one.

2006
MARCH 16

A CELTIC COLLAPSE
A HEAT COMEBACK

THE BOSTON Celtics were not particularly good in the 2005–06 season. When they came to Miami to play the Heat with about a month left in the season, the Celtics were not really playing for much. Meanwhile, the Heat were in the mix for a top seed in the Eastern Conference playoffs.

So, imagine Miami's surprise when the team found itself down by 25 points—61–36—late in the first half. And the Heat were hearing boos from the home fans, too.

No problem. The Heat outscored Boston 71–43 the rest of the way and found a way to pull out a 107–104 win behind 30 points from Dwyane Wade and 26 more from Shaquille O'Neal.

"We learned how to fight tonight," O'Neal said after the game.

Those fighting lessons would be needed later that season, when Miami went on to win its first NBA title.

For the next seven years, the Heat wouldn't muster a comeback that big again. It wasn't until March 2013 when the Heat had another such game, rallying from 27 down in that one to beat Cleveland.

Udonis Haslem hangs on the rim after a dunk against the Boston Celtics on March 16, 2006.

"NO, I AIN'T GOING OUT LIKE THIS."

IT WAS the 2006 NBA Finals. Miami Heat versus the Dallas Mavericks. Dallas wins the first two games of the series at home, Game 1 by 10 points, Game 2 by 14 points. The Mavs were in full control of the series.

And then an unflattering headline came out, suggesting they were unworthy opponents, and that really ticked the Heat off.

But the big slap in the face came when word leaked that Dallas officials were already planning the championship parade.

"It was on," Dwyane Wade said.

Wade had a bad knee and a finger that he wasn't able to bend, and he was still feeling the after-effects of a nasty flu-like virus that he caught during the Eastern Conference finals against Detroit.

The parade talk was the best medicine.

But in Game 3, the parade talk might not have seemed so crazy. The series had shifted back to Miami, and the Mavericks were up by 11 points when Wade checked into the game for one last gasp midway through the fourth quarter. Jason Terry then scored for Dallas, pushing the lead to 13.

That's when Wade uttered the phrase: "No, I ain't going out like this."

He went wild in the last six minutes. Gary Payton made a huge shot from the right wing with nine seconds remaining. The Mavs' last chance was a lob to the rim that Wade broke up. The Heat won Game 3.

And the series was changing.

Miami rolled to a win in Game 4. Before Game 5—the NBA Finals was a 2-3-2 format then, so there were three consecutive games in Miami—the Mavericks moved from their Miami hotel to Fort Lauderdale.

"We knew we were in their head," Wade said. "We knew we had them."

Miami won Game 5 in overtime. Wade scored 43 points, helped by taking 25 free throws. The Mavericks were called for fouls and literally cried foul about it. Wade, to this day, insists the calls were earned.

"Check the tape," Wade says. The Heat took a 3–2 lead back to Dallas. History loomed.

HEAT
3

2006

JUNE 20

ONE SUIT, ONE SHIRT, ONE TIE

Up 3-2 in the 2006 NBA Finals, the Miami Heat headed back to Dallas with two chances to beat the Mavericks for the championship.

Heat coach Pat Riley figured—and insisted—it would only take one.

When the Heat lost Game 2 in Dallas, Riley scrawled a message on the whiteboard in the locker room. "June 20, 2006." That was the date of Game 6. That was the date the Heat would return to win the NBA title, he said.

He was so confident of it that he packed "one suit, one shirt, one tie" for the trip back to Dallas. Two suits weren't necessary. He was going to be there for only one game. And he knew it.

"Riles made us believe," Shaquille O'Neal said.

It was not going to be easy. Heat forward Udonis Haslem had a dislocated shoulder, basically taped into place, and he had fought through pain to guard Dallas star Dirk Nowitzki. Alonzo Mourning played one of the games of his life, leaping over people to block shots. James Posey hit a huge three-pointer from the right corner with about three-and-a-half minutes left.

And after all that, Jason Terry still had a chance to tie the game with a three-pointer. Dwyane Wade got the rebound. He threw the ball into the air. Time expired.

The Miami Heat were world champions. Just like Pat Riley said they would be.

Pat Riley leads the Heat in Game 6 of the 2006 NBA Finals against Dallas.

THE FIRST TITLE, UDONIS CRIED, *AND ANDY DID NOT STAY DRY*

IN CASE Miami Heat CEO Nick Arison ever forgets the team's first championship in 2006—it's pretty certain that will never happen—all he needs for a reminder is a simple glance at his ring finger.

Not the ring. Just his ring finger. There's a scar there to remind him.

In the craziness of Miami's locker-room celebration after winning in Dallas on June 20, 2006, for that season's NBA championship and the franchise's first title, Nick Arison—the son of Heat Managing General Partner Micky Arison—plunged his hand into a tub of ice to grab a Champagne bottle for purposes of drinking, spraying, and probably both.

Small problem. There was a broken bottle in that tub. He sliced his finger open. Someone suggested he needed stitches. Let's put it this way: He was not leaving the party to get stitches.

The final shot of that series was a three-pointer point attempt from Dallas's Jason Terry, which Dwyane Wade rebounded for Miami. Wade threw the ball skyward, just to let the final seconds run off the clock and ensure that the Mavericks wouldn't get a chance at a miracle.

And the party was on. In the locker room, Udonis Haslem, the toughest player on the team, gave in to the emotions and cried. He tried to blame the Champagne burning his eyes, but the tears of joy were real.

Andy Elisburg, the Heat general manager, was one of the last people to get into the joyous locker room. He was on the court and helping get people where they needed to be. He missed the first few Champagne sprays.

Point guard Jason Williams saw Elisburg walk into the locker room. Elisburg was dry. Williams instantly changed that. He sprayed a bottle all over Elisburg, and then someone handed Elisburg his own bottle.

Elisburg didn't spray that one. Instead, he raised it over his head, turned his wrist and dumped the contents all over himself.

Heat forward Udonis Haslem, soaked in Champagne, celebrates the 2006 NBA title inside the Miami locker room.

2006
JUNE 20

WADE WINS NBA FINALS MVP

IN 2006, there was no choice for NBA Finals MVP other than Dwyane Wade after he and the Miami Heat won their first championship.

"The best player in the world," Heat coach Pat Riley would later say, describing Wade's level of play for those two weeks against the Dallas Mavericks.

The Mavs won the first two games, but Wade led the Heat to wins in each of the next four including the title-clincher in Dallas on June 20, 2006.

For the series, Wade averaged 34.7 points, 7.8 rebounds, 3.8 assists, and 2.7 steals per game.

Wade had 42 points in the Game 3 win, 36 in the Game 4 win, 43 in the Game 5 overtime victory, and 36 in the Game 6 title-clinching finale.

DEFENDING THE FIRST TITLE

IT STARTED BAD AND STAYED BAD

THE MIAMI Heat got their 2006 championship rings and then raised the banner for their first title season before facing the Chicago Bulls to open the 2006–07 season.

The pregame was all ceremony.

The game was all . . . something not ceremonial.

Things started coming apart in Game 1 and never really got on track. The Heat lost to the Bulls in that opener 108–66 (yes, 108–66, on ring night). They wound up losing 19 of the season's first 32 games before finally getting some momentum going and getting back to the playoffs with a 44–38 record.

The Bulls awaited them in the playoffs as well. Just like the opener, it was one-sided. Chicago swept the series, and Miami reigned as NBA champions no more in a season that was more frustration than anything else.

Dwyane Wade was limited to 51 games because of injuries. Shaquille O'Neal played in only 40 games that season. It was bad. And what was coming was even worse.

Shaquille O'Neal takes a look at the scoreboard during the 2006–07 Heat season.

President George W. Bush speaks at the White House ceremony welcoming the 2006 NBA champion Miami Heat.

THE NBA CHAMPION MIAMI HEAT VISIT THE WHITE HOUSE

PART OF the perk package for winning the NBA championship: You get invited to the White House.

And on February 27, 2007, the 2006 NBA champion Miami Heat took advantage of that chance.

President George W. Bush welcomed the team, posed for some photos with Shaquille O'Neal and others, and congratulated everybody—including Heat Managing General Partner Micky Arison and his wife Madeleine.

Bush, before his White House days, was an owner of baseball's Texas Rangers.

"As you know, I used to be in pro sports. I never had the pleasure of winning anything," Bush said during the East Room ceremony, a line that drew some laughs.

He timed the pause perfectly. "Must be pretty cool," Bush said, as the laughs got louder.

Bush lauded all facets of the Heat organization, even the equipment managers for ensuring that the team always had what it needed and got to everywhere it needed to get to. He congratulated the spouses of those in the Heat traveling party, telling them that he understood the sacrifices they made because of the daunting schedule of an NBA season. He spoke at length about his fellow Texan O'Neal, detailed how Alonzo Mourning's comeback story from a serious kidney issue was inspiring, raved about Dwyane Wade, and pointed to everything that Pat Riley had done to make the championship happen.

"Pat Riley had a lot to do with this team playing as a team," Bush said. "A team requires a good, solid leader in convincing people to put the team ahead of themselves. And that's exactly what Pat Riley has done. I'd say he's accomplished."

FAREWELL TO RILEY (AS A COACH)

HELLO TO ROCK BOTTOM

PAT RILEY knew the 2007–08 season wasn't going to be an on-court success for the Miami Heat.

He just didn't know how badly it was going to go.

The Heat were pushing the reset button with an eye on the future. That was true. But everything that could have gone wrong that season went wrong as well.

Alonzo Mourning blew out his knee during a game in December 2007 and knew in that moment that his NBA career was over. The Heat went 1–26 in one horrifically dismal 27-game stretch that started on Christmas Day and ended in the last week of February. Shaquille O'Neal, who had been privately telling people for weeks that he was going to get traded, indeed did get moved during that awful losing stretch. He was traded to Phoenix for Shawn Marion and Marcus Banks.

This is how bad it was: The Heat had to win on the final night of the regular season just to get to 15–67 and match the worst record in franchise history. They got that win, in what became Riley's finale as coach.

"I'm a very proud man," Riley said that night, when the 2007–08 season mercifully ended. "But I'm not proud of what we accomplished this year."

He walked off the court when the buzzer sounded and never looked back. Days later, he turned the keys to the head coach's office over to longtime assistant Erik Spoelstra, continuing his long-held belief that the best way to hire a new coach was to promote one from within.

"At first, I didn't even know who Erik was," Riley said.

By then, he did.

Longtime Heat athletic trainer Ron Culp (left) talks with coach Pat Riley during the 2007–08 season.

2008 APRIL

ERIK SPOELSTRA TAKES OVER

IT TOOK Pat Riley nine days to figure out what direction the Miami Heat had go in after the 2007–08 season.

The season—a 15–67 disaster—ended with a win on April 16, 2008. Riley knew that would be his last game as a coach. What he wasn't sure of yet was who would take over. And the rest of the basketball world was guessing as well.

The following Friday, April 25, he told assistant coach Erik Spoelstra of his decision. It was announced widely three days later.

The Spo Era in Miami was set to begin.

Spoelstra was 37, 13 years removed from his first job in the Heat video room, and he was set to be the NBA's youngest coach. Riley saw parallels in their paths. He had been 36 when he first became a head coach after starting his post-playing career as essentially the traveling secretary for the Los Angeles Lakers. Spoelstra's duties in the beginning included making videos for the team Christmas party.

Riley flourished when he got the chance to lead. He was convinced that Spoelstra would do the same.

"It's very rare to have the opportunity to work for one organization for your entire career like I have," Spoelstra said at the time. "It means it's a special organization."

Riley finished his career with 1,210 victories, which was third-most in NBA history at the time behind only Lenny Wilkens and Don Nelson. He had won seven championships, including five as a head coach. (He added two more as an executive in 2012 and 2013.)

But it was the Hall of Fame enshrinement that came his way in 2008 that might have sealed his decision to step away for good and elevate Spoelstra into the top job.

"I think the call from the Hall of Fame did something to me," Riley said. "There was a lot of emotion on that telephone call. When you come to the finish, or you know it's the best time, it's a clean ending."

Erik Spoelstra replaced Pat Riley as Heat coach entering the 2008–09 season.

YEAR ONE OF THE SPO ERA

THERE WERE not much in the way of expectations for new Miami Heat head coach Erik Spoelstra when the 2008–09 season started.

That's exactly the way Heat president (and former coach) Pat Riley wanted it to be.

Spoelstra took over a 15-win team. No pressure there. It was by design in many ways.

When Riley replaced Stan Van Gundy as head coach 21 games into what became the 2005–06 championship season, Spoelstra was deeply entrenched as an assistant coach. One day, Spoelstra loaded a video for Riley to show the team, and Riley decided to surprise him by having him break it down for the players.

Spoelstra didn't know it was coming. He was nervous. Very nervous. It didn't show. He broke down the tape with ease.

He passed Riley's test. Riley never forgot that moment. He was certain about Spoelstra from that point forward.

"When I turned over the team to him in 2008, I knew I was done," Riley said. "We traded (Shaquille O'Neal) and I took that team to the bottom because I wanted the No. 1 pick in the draft."

The Heat didn't get the No. 1 pick. They got the No. 2 pick in the draft lottery and used it to select Michael Beasley. But everything else went according to plan.

Riley took a break in the 2007–08 season to scout college players, but didn't want to make Spoelstra the interim coach in his absence because he didn't want him to have a bad first experience in the job. He wanted to make sure the time was right to turn the reins over.

Spoelstra proved him right.

The Heat won 43 games in Spoelstra's first season and returned to the playoffs, while Dwyane Wade won the NBA scoring title. He had 55 points against New York, 50 at Orlando, 50 against Utah, and a 48-point effort capped by his running three-pointer at the buzzer of double overtime to beat Chicago on March 9, 2009.

Wade shouted "this is my house" after that shot, as he leaped onto the table where Heat Managing General Partner Micky Arison sits during games.

The house was in order again, too.

2009
APRIL 12

WADE SCORES 55

DWYANE WADE showed up for work on April 12, 2009, in a mood. His Miami Heat teammates couldn't figure it out. He really wasn't saying much of anything, which wasn't like him.

Evidently, he was just focused.

And then he dropped 55 points on the New York Knicks.

It was the highest-scoring game of Wade's career, a masterpiece that led the Heat past the Knicks 122–105.

Wade shot 19-for-30 from the field. He made six three-pointers, a career-best at the time. He checked out of the game with 1:06 left, just one point shy of Glen Rice's franchise record. Heat coach Erik Spoelstra knew it, but felt leaving Wade out there for a meaningless final minute would be too risky with the playoffs so close.

"He's broken every other record," Spoelstra said that night. "Let's leave one of them to Glen Rice."

Wade scored for the final time with 5:31 remaining. The Knicks had no answers.

"When he is hot," New York's Al Harrington said, "you are in for a long night."

Dwyane Wade shoots against New York's David Lee during a game in 2009. Wade finished with 55 points.

TIM HARDAWAY'S JERSEY TAKES ITS PLACE IN THE RAFTERS

TIM HARDAWAY could do it all. He could score. He could shoot. He could pass. He could defend. He battled, dove for loose balls, fought with opponents, even fought with referees. And when all else failed he would use his "killer crossover" dribble to make a play.

A Miami Heat legend, for certain.

And on October 28, 2009, the team made it official.

Hardaway's No. 10 jersey was retired that night, the second in team history to get that distinction after Alonzo Mourning's. The Heat surprised Hardaway by having a pair of his "Run TMC" teammates from Golden State—Mitch Richmond and Chris Mullin—there for the festivities, which only added to how special the night was for Hardaway.

"Tonight, I stand before you truly humble and grateful," Hardaway said.

Heat President Pat Riley never hid the fact that Hardaway was one of his favorites, and he beamed when seeing Hardaway's eyes well up that night.

"It's another great moment," Riley said. "I would say from the year 2006 until now, we've had a couple of incredible moments. Both of them are hanging from the rafters, our world championship banner that we're so proud of—and there's more of those in store for the future—and of course Alonzo Mourning last year, one of the anchors of this franchise."

Heat legend Tim Hardaway's jersey is lifted to the rafters in a 2009 ceremony.

Heat coach Erik Spoelstra (left) enjoys a moment with assistant coaches Chad Kammerer, Bob McAdoo, and David Fizdale.

YEAR TWO OF SPO

GETTING READY FOR WHAT'S NEXT

ERIK SPOELSTRA was settling into the job nicely when the 2009–10 Miami Heat season came along.

That was year two of the Spoelstra Era, and the Heat raised the win total some more, this time getting to 47 wins and returning to the playoffs. The on-court product was good. But everyone in the organization was still laser-focused on the bigger goal, the summer of 2010, the reason why the Heat had self-inflicted a whole ton of losses in 2007–08 to help ensure everything got aligned for that summer.

From the start of the 2006–07 season through the end of the 2009–10 season, the Heat had 43 different players appear in at least one game. Most were long gone by the time the 2010–11 season started; only seven of the 43 were still there.

When the 2009–10 season ended, Miami had a ton to offer. A good team, again. Wade was at his peak. Spoelstra was proven. The Heat had more salary-cap space than any other team in the NBA. They were the only team that had the financial ability to put three stars—oh, hypothetically, let's say Dwyane Wade, LeBron James, and Chris Bosh—on the same roster. A series of one-year deals, smart spending, and diligent strategy made all that possible.

The Heat bet on themselves.

"I had a gut feeling, that whole year, that we were going to be in a great position to offer something to three free agents," Heat President Pat Riley said. "And I knew they wouldn't be able to turn it down. I didn't know which three we were getting, but I knew we were going to get three of them."

BACK IN DALLAS

WADE PUTS ON AN ALL-STAR MVP SHOW

SOMETHING ABOUT Dallas brought out the best in Dwyane Wade.

The Miami Heat's first championship was in 2006, when they clinched in Dallas with Wade winning NBA Finals MVP honors after going on a four-game tear to lead the comeback to the title.

And in 2010, in Arlington, Texas—the home of the Dallas Cowboys—Wade put on a dazzling show before a record crowd in the All-Star Game.

Before an announced attendance of 108,713, Wade scored 28 points and took home MVP honors as the Eastern Conference topped the Western Conference 141–139. Chris Bosh—who would join the Heat a few months later—made the winning free throws with five seconds left. And that was fitting; Bosh is a Dallas native.

"I've had a little luck in Dallas," Wade said that night. "Of course, 2006 is very, very memorable. Something that I dreamed of doing for a long time, winning the NBA championship and I was lucky enough and blessed enough to win the MVP award there. To come and do it again is special."

The last question he took at his All-Star Game news conference was the one he'd been waiting all night to answer. Wade was teammates with LeBron James in that All-Star Game. Had he thought about being teammates with him for more than one day a year?

"I was wondering what took so long for that question," he said. "Yeah, we can dream, can't we? I dream."

Five months later, the world found out that the dream would become a reality.

Heat guard Dwyane Wade displays the 2010 NBA All-Star Game MVP trophy.

Dwyane Wade and Boston forward Paul Pierce embrace after the Celtics eliminated the Heat from the 2010 NBA playoffs.

THE PROMISE—OR THE VOW

THE 2009–10 Miami Heat season had just ended. The Heat had been eliminated in five games in a Round 1 matchup against the Boston Celtics. And as he did more than 1,000 times in his career, Dwyane Wade emerged after the game for his question-and-answer session with the media.

This one was not like almost all the others.

Maybe he was foreshadowing. Maybe he was promising. Maybe he was threatening. Only Wade knows for certain. But that night in Boston, Wade let Heat Nation and the rest of the basketball world know exactly what he was thinking.

"This will be my last first-round exit for a while," Wade said that night.

Fast forward two-and-a-half months. That would be the next time the world got to see Wade wearing his No. 3 Heat jersey again. It was July 8, 2010, the night that he, LeBron James, and Chris Bosh pulled on Miami uniforms and went out to meet the crowd at what was then called AmericanAirlines Arena for the rally to celebrate their decisions to team up and play together for the Heat.

Miami's Big Three era was about to begin. Wade was right. He didn't have a first-round exit for many years after that.

James promised championships (and delivered, twice). Bosh called the chance to be in Miami "a golden opportunity." Wade helped orchestrate the whole thing with what he said in Boston after that playoff loss.

It wasn't a throwaway comment. It was a vow.

One of Dwyane Wade's pregame traditions included doing a pull-up on the rim.

THE (FIRST) DECISIONS

WADE STAYS, CHRIS BOSH COMES TO MIAMI

DWYANE WADE got a pretty good fireworks show on July 4, 2010. It was in the form of a phone call.

The caller was Chris Bosh.

"I'm feeling Miami," Bosh told Wade.

The Miami Heat didn't know it yet, but they were on their way to an entirely new era. The Big Three era was set to take flight in South Florida.

This is how it went down: Wade, Bosh, and LeBron James were all parts—the biggest parts, probably—of one of the most-anticipated free-agent summers in NBA history. Would Wade stay in Miami? Where was Bosh going? Would James leave Cleveland for New York or Miami or stay home?

Wade had already told the Heat that he wanted to stay, but that he needed a star alongside him—preferably Bosh or James. The dream was both. Wade would have settled for one. And when Bosh made that phone call, Wade knew he was staying in Miami.

"There's a lot of talented players in this league," Wade said. "But you want to look at players that complement my game, and Chris and LeBron are two of those guys. I had a decision to make. Chris had a decision to make. It wasn't a lock that he would come to Miami. So, I had a lot to think about."

Bosh said it just made sense. Wade had already won a title. Bosh was an All-Star. He and Wade came into the league one pick apart in 2003—Bosh at No. 4, Wade at No. 5. They were ready to team up.

And then they waited to see if the duo would become a trio.

Pat Riley, Erik Spoelstra, LeBron James, Dwyane Wade, Chris Bosh, and Micky Arison at the news conference announcing the star trio as new Heat teammates in 2010.

THE DECISION
LEBRON JAMES TAKES HIS TALENTS TO SOUTH BEACH

On July 8, 2010, LeBron James was finally ready to reveal his free agency decision. A 75-minute television show was hastily arranged on ESPN; the NBA didn't want it to happen, but not even Commissioner David Stern could stop it.

James went to Greenwich, Connecticut, to the Boys and Girls Club there for the show, which was to be aired live. He let the Cleveland Cavaliers know shortly before the 9 p.m. start time of his decision. He let a few others know as well, including Dwyane Wade.

And at 9:27 p.m. Eastern, James told the world.

"I'm going to take my talents to South Beach and join the Miami Heat," he told show host Jim Gray.

"Miami Heat. That was the conclusion you woke up with this morning?" Gray asked.

"That was the conclusion I woke up with this morning," James said.

Inside Prime 112, a Miami Beach steakhouse, Wade—who kept the secret—screamed in delight at a watch party. It didn't take long for Heat fans to line some of Miami's busiest streets, like Calle Ocho in the Little Havana neighborhood, and start banging pots and pans together in celebration. (It's a Miami thing. It's a big deal when that happens.)

James got on a plane after the show and flew to Miami International Airport, where a number of Heat staff and executives including Pat Riley were waiting to greet his private jet. Police guessed that about 2,000 fans were outside the fence when he got there. Some people tailed the SUV that whisked him from the airport to Miami Beach for a celebration party.

James and his talents were in Miami. His career was about to change. So was Miami. So was Heat basketball.

YES. WE. DID.

LET'S CLEAR up a misconception here: No, LeBron James did not predict the Miami Heat would win eight NBA championships when he joined the team.

Not really, anyway.

At the welcome party for James, Dwyane Wade, and Chris Bosh, James famously said "not two, not three, not four, not five, not six, not seven" when the on-stage conversation moderated by Heat broadcasters Eric Reid and Jose Paneda turned to how the group came together to win multiple championships.

James was simply following Reid's lead when the television voice of the team told the trio that he knew they came together to win titles. "Not one. Championships," Reid said. "LeBron, tell us about that."

And that's when "not two, not three, not four, not five, not six, not seven" happened.

They packed the arena with about 13,000 people that night, and police estimated another 10,000 who couldn't get the tickets were outside the building. James, wearing his white Heat uniform for the first time, arrived with Wade and Bosh on

LeBron James greets the fans at his welcome party after joining the Miami Heat in 2010.

the stage after they were hoisted in a forklift and let out a big scream.

"We know what the fans want," James said.

"It's still surreal, man," Wade said. "Me, Chris, and 'Bron. We ready. We want to go to the gym now."

At the rally, which was announced a few hours before it started and for which tickets disappeared in less than 60 minutes, fans were given posters with James, Wade, and Bosh together in Heat uniforms.

"Yes. We. Did." was the slogan on those posters.

"All three of these gentlemen up here are going to be here for a long time and they're going to be here for a long time for us to enjoy, thoroughly enjoy," Heat President Pat Riley said.

Fans celebrate at the party welcoming LeBron James, Chris Bosh, and Dwyane Wade to Miami.

Chris Bosh (left) lets out a scream as he, Dwyane Wade, and LeBron James make their debut appearance as teammates in Miami in 2010.

Udonis Haslem nearly left the Heat in free agency in 2010, before leaving money on the table and re-signing with Miami.

GIVING BACK

SO HASLEM WOULDN'T GO AWAY

DWYANE WADE and Udonis Haslem grew extremely close in their first seven years together with the Miami Heat. They dressed alike for a while (though neither wants to admit that now). They drove the same cars a couple of times; the Bentleys didn't match perfectly, but close enough. They had big chains for a while and thought they were rock stars.

They also had real bonds. Both became parents at a young age. Both had parents who struggled with addiction. They relied on each other for advice. The friendship was real and was deep.

And in 2010, they almost had to part ways.

The Heat were keeping Wade and getting LeBron James and Chris Bosh. That meant some players couldn't be kept; the team just was running out of cap space and other mechanisms by which to sign people. The Denver Nuggets knew this and offered Haslem a five-year, $34 million contract. For Haslem, that was life-changing money. He made his mind up. He was leaving Miami.

He was on the way to Pat Riley's office to deliver the news and his agent, Henry Thomas, asked for a few minutes alone with Riley first. Turns out, Wade was going to give back some money. James and Bosh took a bit less than the maximums they were offered as well. The Heat scraped together enough to offer Haslem a $20 million deal.

He took it. He never left.

WHEN THE BIG THREE ARRIVED, SO DID BIG BUSINESS

THE BIG Three of LeBron James, Dwyane Wade, and Chris Bosh joining up as teammates with the Miami Heat in the summer of 2010 also meant big business—for the team, and for other businesses in South Florida.

It was craziness, plain and simple.

Forget tickets: they were always going to sell. But some of the other things that happened, those might not necessarily have been expected.

"What this is going to bring to the city of Miami, what winning brings period, what excitement brings, is togetherness," Wade said. "Everyone wants to be together. Everyone wants to be a part of it."

There was a LeBron Burger at one restaurant, topped with onion rings (as in championship rings) and jalapenos (for heat, of course).

A spa on Miami Beach offered the "LeBroyal Treatment." Another hotel on Miami Beach had a Heat suite available; booking that room also came with the opportunity to use a Ferrari and access James's favorite snacks. Another hotel in downtown Miami offered guests cookies decorated like basketballs.

"The interest is clearly out there," said Eric Woolworth, the Heat president of business operations.

Chris Bosh, Dwyane Wade, and LeBron James formed what was called the Big Three era in Miami.

The early days of LeBron James's tenure with the Miami Heat were not without challenges.

BUMPGATE

THE START of the Big Three era was not perfect. Far from it. LeBron James, Chris Bosh, and Dwyane Wade were not instantly unbeatable.

Some might say the road was bumpy.

Welcome to Bumpgate.

Let's explain: On November 27, 2010, the Miami Heat were playing in Dallas against the Mavericks. They were about to lose. Miami would fall to 9–8 with the loss.

Heat coach Erik Spoelstra called time-out and had a full head of steam when he stomped onto the court in the third quarter. James walked past him. His right shoulder bumped Spoelstra's right shoulder. Was it intentional? Probably. Sure seemed it, anyway.

That was Bumpgate.

"The infamous 'Bumpgate,'" Spoelstra said. "That was a good starting moment for LeBron and I, just from the standpoint that we both realized, 'Hey, this is bizarre, the spotlight and the story lines that are developing with this team.' The two of us seemed to be a lightning rod for it. We understood we're in this together and the only way we'd all figure this out is if we got on the same page."

So, that's what they did.

Meetings were held. Heat President Pat Riley made clear that Spoelstra was the coach. Spoelstra and James had a one-on-one meeting to talk things out and find out more about one another.

The Heat went 21–1 in their next 22 games. They were off and running.

"I knew my communication with the head coach had to become better," James said.

Clearly, that happened.

JAMES RETURNS TO CLEVELAND
AS AN OPPONENT

TO PROPERLY explain how high the tensions were in Cleveland on December 2, 2010, when the Miami Heat visited the Cavaliers in LeBron James's first game there as an opponent, consider how the Cavs' mascot handled the evening.

Moondog, the mascot, wore a bulletproof vest.

It was unpleasant, to say the least. James got booed, taunted, yelled at. The Heat bench had things thrown their way. It was one of the ugliest pregame scenes that anyone in the NBA could remember. It was not "Welcome home, LeBron." It was the opposite.

James ignored it all. He scored 38 points and sat out the fourth quarter, and the Heat rolled to a 118–90 win.

"I have the utmost respect for these fans," James said. "It's nothing personal."

James had left the previous summer for Miami, taking his "talents to South Beach." In time, Cleveland got over it. By December 2010, five months removed from it all, no, Cavs fans had not gotten over it. Not even close.

"I don't want to apologize," James said that night. "I think my intentions were not to hurt anyone. My intentions were solely on my kids during that whole process. I always say, decisions I make, I live with them. There's always ways you can correct them or ways you can do them better. At the end of the day, I live with them. I'm satisfied and happy right now."

Fans in Cleveland watch LeBron James's traditional pregame powder toss in his first game there as an opponent in 2010.

LeBron James celebrates a playoff win over the Boston Celtics during the 2011 NBA postseason.

THE FIRST BIG THREE PLAYOFF RUN

4-1, 4-1, AND 4-1

THE FIRST three playoff series that LeBron James, Dwyane Wade, and Chris Bosh played together as the Big Three of the Miami Heat went just about according to plan in the spring of 2011.

They rolled through the Eastern Conference Finals. They beat Philadelphia 4–1 in Round 1, Boston 4–1 in Round 2, and Chicago 4–1 in the Eastern Conference Finals. The Bulls actually put Miami into a bit of a spot by winning Game 1 of that East title series; the Heat took the next four games and even rallied from 12 points down in the final 3:36 of Game 5 to clinch the crown.

Chicago led 76–64 when James got fouled with 3:36 remaining. The Heat outscored Chicago 19–4 the rest of the way, taking the lead on a basket by James with 29.5 seconds left. Bosh pushed the lead to three with a pair of free throws, and James blocked Derrick Rose's potentially game-tying three-pointer as time expired.

The Heat, in year one of the Big Three, were headed to the NBA Finals.

RILEY WINS NBA EXECUTIVE OF THE YEAR

LANDING THE Big Three in the summer of 2010 earned Miami Heat President Pat Riley a big prize in 2011.

Riley was the league's executive of the year that season, sharing the honor with Chicago Bulls general manager Gar Forman. Both Riley and Forman received 11 votes from the panel of 30 team executives, one from each of the league's franchises.

It was the first time the Heat had someone win that particular award.

It was Riley's 16th season with the Heat and came after he helped plan and execute one of the biggest offseason player hauls in league history. Not only did the Heat keep Dwyane Wade, but they added LeBron James and Chris Bosh to form the core of a team that would go on to win four consecutive Eastern Conference titles and two NBA championships.

Through 2025, the Heat had not won the executive of the year award again.

Pat Riley, flanked by members of the Heat front office, was the co-winner of the 2011 NBA executive of the year award.

2011
JUNE

THE FIRST BIG THREE FINALS END WITH DALLAS WINNING TITLE

IT WAS not to be in 2011 for the Miami Heat. They made the NBA Finals in the first season of the Big Three era that brought LeBron James, Dwyane Wade, and Chris Bosh together. They even took a 2–1 series lead over the Dallas Mavericks in those finals.

And then it was all Dallas the rest of the way. The Mavericks won the final three games of the series and not only won the championship but did it in Game 6 on Miami's home floor—just like what the Heat did against Dallas five years earlier.

Wade averaged 26.5 points in the series, Bosh averaged 18.5, and James averaged 17.8. James was widely criticized for how he didn't take over the series and for often deferring to teammates in the biggest moments.

"So much had gone on with that series and the whole season," James said a year later. "I played too much to prove people wrong, instead of just playing my game and doing what needs to be done."

He vowed to figure things out and come back better. That's exactly what he did.

Dallas's Dirk Nowitzki celebrates as the Mavericks close in on the 2006 NBA title by winning the clinching Game 6 in Miami.

DALLAS
41
NBA
NBA TV
SPALDING
The Finals
WADS
PAYTON
14

Heat President Pat Riley poses with forward Shane Battier during a news conference announcing the free agent signing.

WELCOME TO MIAMI, *SHANE BATTIER*

WHEN LEBRON James and Chris Bosh came to Miami, the basketball world seemed split into two pieces: Those who liked the Heat, and everybody else.

Shane Battier, then of the Memphis Grizzlies, was in group B.

Battier was already an accomplished NBA player at that point in his career, one of the league's smartest guys, one of the league's most-respected guys. And he didn't love the idea of James and Bosh heading to Miami.

He watched Miami lose to Dallas in the 2011 NBA Finals, and by then he was fully sold on the potential of what the Heat could be.

"I had a new least favorite team, like everyone else in the Western world," Battier said. "I was like everybody else; I wanted to see how the egos would mesh. The first year it was clunky. I didn't take delight in that they lost, but I wanted to see how they were going to figure this thing out. It didn't take long to realize they were going to win at least one title together, no question."

But how?

Changes had to be made. And this is where Battier comes in.

He was signed by the Heat before the lockout-shortened 2011–12 season and instantly became a key upgrade for Miami.

And the way he joined the team remains classic. Battier made his announcement on the social media site then known as Twitter, parroting Heat fan and music icon Jimmy Buffett when he made the decision.

"The Lockout gave me a lot of time to consider what was important to me at this stage of my life and career," he tweeted. "Over the last week, I've played out every scenario in my head over and over. It always came back to one thing for me: a winning role.

"I would like to quote the great poet Jimmy Buffett and take my chances 'Trying to Reason with Hurricane Season.'"

Hurricane Shane was about to hit Miami.

JAMES WINS NBA MVP

LEBRON JAMES'S first Miami Heat season had MVP-type numbers: 26.7 points, 7.5 rebounds, and 7 assists per game. But the MVP award for that 2010–11 season went to Chicago Bulls guard Derrick Rose, in a runaway vote.

James finished third that year. Rose had a superb season, without question, but there was sentiment that voters held James's decision to come to Miami—and how he announced "The Decision"—against him in the balloting.

A year later, all that was evidently forgotten.

James became the first Heat player to win MVP, taking the award in the 2011–12 season after averaging 27.1 points, 7.9 rebounds, and 6.2 assists per game. He got 85 first-place votes, winning by a wide margin over Oklahoma City's Kevin Durant. James and Durant would meet up in that season's NBA Finals as well, with the Heat topping the Thunder in five games.

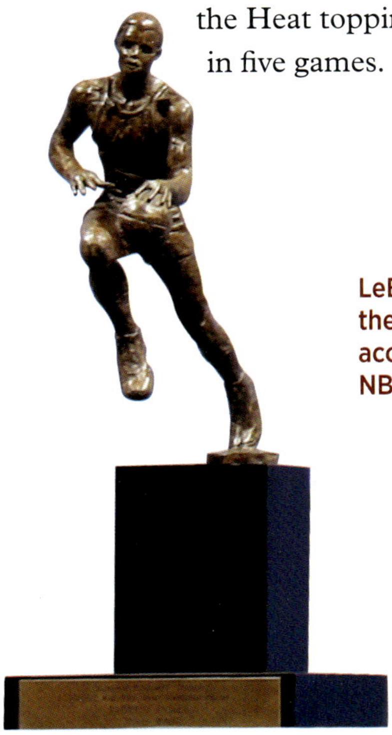

LeBron James of the Miami Heat accepts the 2012 NBA MVP award.

2012

JUNE 7

WITH "THE LOOK," JAMES HAS A VIRAL MOMENT IN GAME 6 AT BOSTON

THE MIAMI Heat lost Game 5 of the 2012 Eastern Conference finals at home to the Boston Celtics, falling into a 3–2 series hole and having to go on the road to save the season.

The stakes were enormous. The Heat lost the 2011 NBA Finals to Dallas. They were about to lose in the East finals a year later. There was talk of breaking up the Big Three of James, Dwyane Wade, and Chris Bosh.

No problem, James said.

The Heat were stuck in traffic and got to the arena in Boston late for Game 6. Pregame routines were disrupted. No problem, James said again. And on the night where he went viral for The Look—cameras catching James staring with a very focused look on his face—James played one of the best games of his legendary career.

He missed his first shot. He made his next 12 shots. The outcome was never in doubt. The Celtics had no answers, and Miami won 98–79 behind a 45-point, 15-rebound, five-assist performance from the best player in the world.

"I felt like I was aggressive from the opening tip, and the guys continued to find me. I tried to keep it going," James said. "I felt like that a few times in this postseason. And it's a great feeling to be in when you feel like everything you put up is going in. But you just can't . . . you can never let go."

The Heat didn't let go. They were going home instead—for Game 7.

BOSTON CELTICS 1964 WORLD CHAMPIONS
BOSTON CELTICS 1957 WORLD CHAMPIONS
1959 WORLD CHAMPIONS
AMES AREN'T SO AWAY AN
S AREN'T SO AWAY ANYMORE
PIERCE
34
MIAMI
6
jetBlue
SYLVANIA
Gillette
ARBELLA INSURANCE
11
FG 25/50 3PT 5/10 TO 7 STL 6 AST 8 REB 27

HEAT
1

HEAT VS. BOSTON

A CLASSIC GAME 7

THE FINAL score of Game 7 of the 2012 Eastern Conference Finals between the Miami Heat and Boston Celtics was not in any way indicative of how the game really was.

Heat 101, Celtics 88 suggests it really was a 13-point game.

Technically, yes. Actually, not even close.

The game had 20 lead changes and 10 ties. Boston—which had won Game 5 in Miami to take a 3–2 series lead—held an 11-point lead late in the first half. For 13 minutes of the second half, it was a heavyweight fight, the two teams going shot for shot, knockout punch for knockout punch, with a berth in the NBA Finals on the line.

That's not hyperbole. It really happened.

Shane Battier took a pass from Dwyane Wade and connected on a three-pointer to get the Heat within 59–57 with 8:06 left in the third quarter.

From there, the chess match went like this:

—Wade scores, game tied
—Kevin Garnett scores, Boston by two
—LeBron James scores, tied
—Rajon Rondo free throw, Boston by one
—Wade scores, Miami by one
—Garnett scores, Boston by one
—Mario Chalmers scores, Miami by one
—Paul Pierce makes two free throws, Boston by one
—James scores, Miami by one
—Wade makes a free throw, Miami by two
—Rondo scores, tied
—Chalmers scores, Miami by two
—Rondo scores, tied
—James makes free throw, Miami by one
—Rondo makes a three, Boston by two
—Chris Bosh scores, tied
—Rondo scores, Boston by two
—Bosh makes a three, Miami by one
—Garnett scores, Boston by one
—Wade scores, Miami by one
—Pierce scores, Boston by one
—James three-point play, Miami by two
—Ray Allen makes a three, Boston by one
—James scores, Miami by one

And then, at last, the Celtics didn't answer. Bosh made a three-pointer with 7:17 left for a four-point Heat lead. The lead never got smaller than that again. Wade sealed it with a three-point play with 2:53 left, and Miami headed back to the NBA Finals.

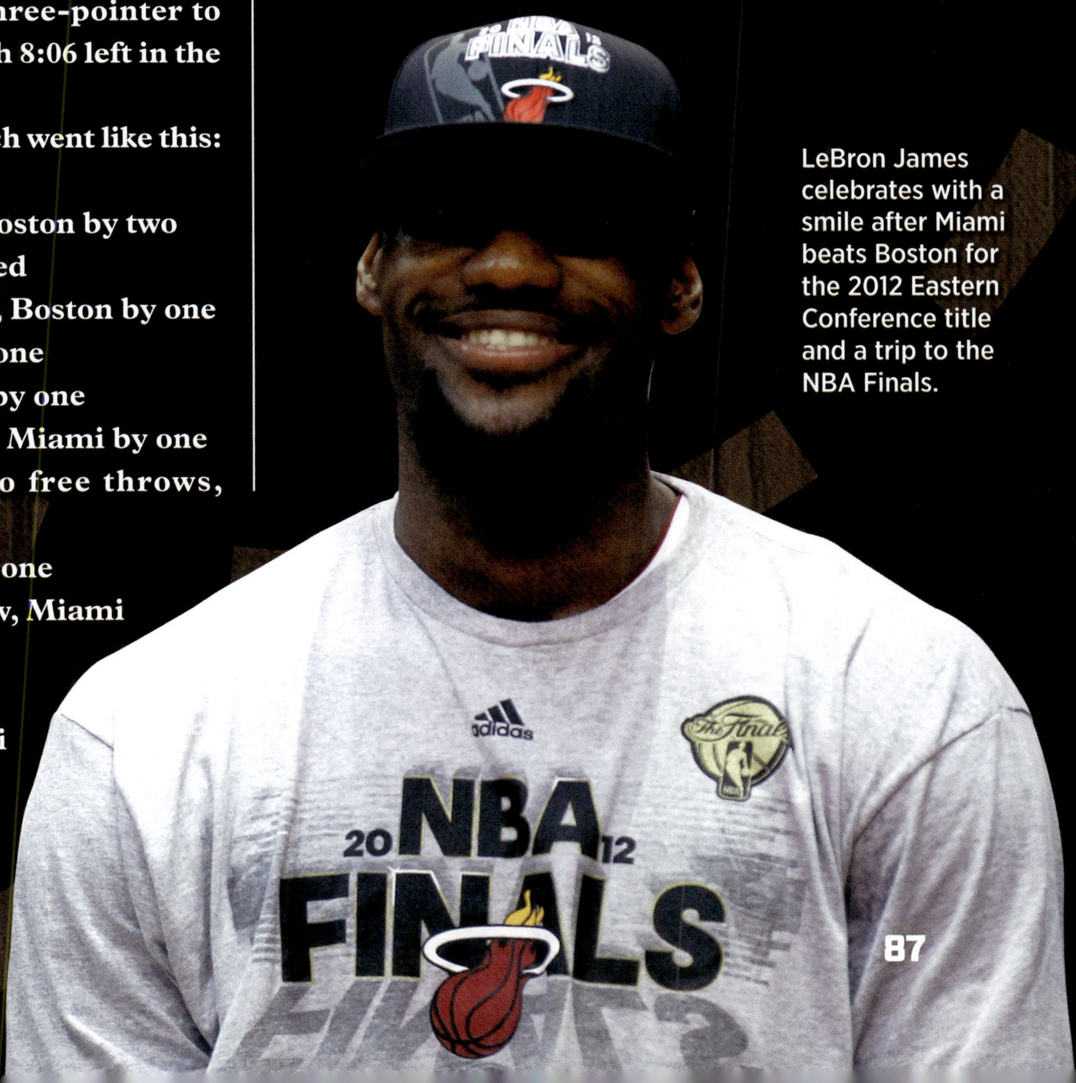

LeBron James celebrates with a smile after Miami beats Boston for the 2012 Eastern Conference title and a trip to the NBA Finals.

MARIO CHALMERS COMES UP CLUTCH YET AGAIN

WHEN GAME 4 of the 2012 NBA Finals ended, Dwyane Wade was trying to get Mario Chalmers's attention as they made their way to the Miami Heat locker room. They were in Championship Alley, the name for the hallway that links the Heat locker room with the court. Chalmers was a few feet ahead of Wade, not hearing Wade call his name. "Mario . . . [expletive]," Wade famously yelled, the moment caught by the ABC cameras.

Chalmers had heard Wade, LeBron James, and others direct . . . um, bad words, we'll call them . . . his way before. That night, they were the highest of praise. When James cramped up late in Game 4 against the Oklahoma City Thunder, Chalmers took over. He had 12 points in the fourth quarter, helping the Heat take a 3–1 lead in the series with a 104–98 win.

"No matter what, no matter how tough we are on him, he actually thinks he's the best player on this team and that's a gift and a curse," Wade said. "But tonight it was a gift for us because he never gets down on himself, he always believes, 'Find me, I can make a shot. I can make a play.' He was huge for us."

Chalmers had largely struggled in the series until that night.

"I didn't lose any confidence," Chalmers said.

It was just another example of Chalmers coming up big, just like he did for Kansas with an overtime-forcing three-pointer in the final seconds of the 2008 NCAA title game against Memphis. Chalmers won a college ring that night. Two nights after his Game 4 heroics, he would be an NBA champion as well, with the Heat closing out the Thunder in five games.

Heat point guard Mario Chalmers had a sensational Game 4 of the 2012 NBA Finals, moving Miami one win from that season's championship.

Heat President Pat Riley won the 2012 Chuck Daly Lifetime Achievement Award from the National Basketball Coaches Association.

RILEY WINS NBCA LIFETIME ACHIEVEMENT AWARD

PAT RILEY and Chuck Daly were rivals as coaches. They became close friends. Riley wept openly at Daly's funeral in 2009.

And in 2012, they were linked yet again.

That was when the National Basketball Coaches Association selected Riley as that year's recipient of the Chuck Daly Lifetime Achievement Award. That award celebrates Daly's "standard of integrity, competitive excellence and tireless promotion" of the game.

"This is not an award," Riley said. "This is something somebody bestows on you. I'm very honored that the coaches association would do this."

For Riley, winning that award in 2012 was particularly special—since it was the 20th anniversary of the US Olympic team called the Dream Team, the first one filled with NBA players that rolled to gold at the Barcelona Games with Daly as its coach.

"I think the perspective was very clear what that team was and what that team was about," Riley said. "He had absolute confidence being around these types of players, tremendous confidence and challenged them in such a way that I don't think anybody else could have challenged them."

NBA FINALS, GAME 5

JAMES BECOMES A CHAMPION

FINALLY.

June 21, 2012, was the day when LeBron James, the No. 1 pick in the 2003 NBA draft, someone who was a national brand before even leaving high school, finally became an NBA champion.

The final numbers: James had 26 points, 11 rebounds, and 13 assists. He led the Heat to a not-as-close-as-the-score-seemed 121–106 win over the Oklahoma City Thunder in Game 5 of the NBA Finals. The Heat won the series 4–1.

"This right here is the happiest day of my life," James told ESPN's Stuart Scott in the on-court celebration, as he looked out at 20,000 delirious Heat fans in the stands. "It's the happiest day of my life. And I wouldn't want to spend it with nobody else in the world besides my teammates. These fans, oh my God, you guys are unbelievable. And this is a dream come true."

When a whistle sounded to stop the clock with 3:01 left in the fourth, James put his head against Chris Bosh's chest, taking a moment to compose himself before the party got started. He hopped up and down on the sideline before the confetti fell, then beelined over to Thunder star Kevin Durant for a hug and some kind words when time expired.

And then James gave the infamous quote, the one he'd waited nine years to say.

"It's about damn time," he said. "It's about damn time."

Udonis Haslem dumps Gatorade over the head of Heat coach Erik Spoelstra in celebration of Miami winning the 2012 NBA championship.

2012 NBA CHAMPIONS
CHAMPIONS
2·0·1·2 NBA CHAMPIONS
adidas
2·0·1·2 N·B·A
CHAMPIONS

JAMES WINS NBA FINALS MVP

THIS WAS LeBron James's 2011–12 season for the Miami Heat: MVP, NBA champion, and then to cap it all off, NBA Finals MVP.

James pulled off the clean sweep of coveted prizes that season (and would do it again a year later). He controlled the 2012 NBA Finals from start to finish, averaged 28.6 points in the series, and carried the Heat to a five-game win over the Oklahoma City Thunder.

It was James's first championship and the second in Heat history.

James was remarkably consistent in that series: 30 points on 46 percent shooting in Game 1, 32 points on 46 percent shooting in Game 2, 29 points on 48 percent shooting in Game 3, 26 points on 50 percent shooting in Game 4, and 26 points on 47 percent shooting in Game 5. The Heat lost Game 1, then won the next four games for the title.

And James finished it with style: He had a triple-double in the finale, adding 11 rebounds and 13 assists to those 26 points.

LeBron James had a triple-double in Game 5 of the 2012 NBA Finals, locking up a title and his selection as Finals MVP.

Heat coach Erik Spoelstra (right) smiles at the news conference announcing Miami's signing of guard Ray Allen in 2012.

WELCOME TO MIAMI, *RAY ALLEN*

WHEN DWYANE Wade heard the news a few days after the Miami Heat won the 2012 NBA championship, he stopped dead in his tracks and asked the person he was talking with to repeat what was just said.

"Wait. We got Ray Allen?"

That's what the message was at that moment, and just like that, a championship team got even better.

The Heat had to get past Allen and Boston in the 2011 playoffs, then win two elimination games against Boston in the 2012 playoffs—including Game 6 of the Eastern Conference finals on the Celtics' home floor.

"You come into the summer, and you don't know what potentially can happen," Allen said at his introductory news conference with the Heat. "And you take the process a step at a time, try to figure out what's best for you and your family. And here I sit."

Miami raised its championship banner at home, against Boston, so Allen's debut with his new team came against his old team.

He made an immediate impact: 19 points on just seven shots from the floor—plus a pair of free throws after technical fouls on the Celtics in the fourth quarter—and the Heat won 120–107.

"There's only a handful of players, really, in this league that absolutely strike fear into their opponent," Heat coach Erik Spoelstra said. "And Ray is one of those players."

THE NBA CHAMPIONS GO TO THE WHITE HOUSE, AGAIN

LEBRON JAMES was standing next to President Barack Obama in the White House, looking at his team surrounding them.

It almost seemed like that was the moment in which James realized the Heat essentially represented a cross-section of the United States.

"We came from Chicago and Dallas, Texas, and Michigan and Ohio and South Dakota, Miami," James said. "I mean, we in the White House right now. This is like, 'Hey, Mama, I made it.'"

Indeed, he had. The Miami Heat made it to the White House to commemorate winning the 2012 NBA championship, the traditional honor that many professional and college title–winning teams get in the US.

Obama—who does not hide his basketball fandom—reveled in the chance to spend some time with the Heat, their coaches, their ownership, their leadership, and some staff.

"Today I'm honored to welcome a little up and coming basketball team, the world champion Miami Heat," Obama said. "For many teams that come here, this is a lot of cameras in one place. It's a little overwhelming. But for the Heat, this is what practice looks like."

The group spent a couple of hours at the White House that day, getting a behind-the-scenes tour and then taking part in the more-public ceremony when Obama was presented with gifts from the Heat.

"This team traveled a long road to get to where they are," Obama said. "In 2011, the Heat got all the way to the finals, only to come up short. But when you fall, the real test is whether you can ignore the naysayers, pick yourself up and come back stronger. And that's true in basketball, but it's also true in life. That's exactly what these guys did. That team mentality, with everybody doing their part, is what finally put the Heat over the top."

THE 27-GAME WINNING STREAK

THE MIAMI Heat beat the Toronto Raptors on Super Bowl Sunday, February 3, 2013. Little did they know they were starting what became a Super Streak.

As in, the second-longest winning streak in NBA history.

For nearly two months, the Heat were unbeatable—winning 27 consecutive games, a stretch that ended six games short of the 33-game streak by the 1971–72 Los Angeles Lakers.

The Heat beat Philadelphia three times during the streak and went 2–0 against Charlotte, Orlando, Cleveland, Atlanta, and Toronto.

They rallied from seven double-digit deficits during the streak.

LeBron James, Chris Andersen, Mario Chalmers, and Norris Cole played in all 27 games. Ray Allen, Udonis Haslem, and Shane Battier played in 26. Dwyane Wade and Chris Bosh both played in 25.

James led the Heat during the streak, averaging 27 points per game while Wade averaged 22.8.

A look at that streak:

FEBRUARY 3, 2013: HEAT 100, TORONTO 85

LeBron James scored 30 points, Chris Bosh added 28, Dwyane Wade scored 23, and the Heat held Toronto to 35 second-half points to pull off a come-from-behind victory.

FEBRUARY 4, 2013: HEAT 99, CHARLOTTE 94

James scored 31, Bosh scored 23, and Wade added 20 as Miami struggled at times but held off the Bobcats.

LeBron James had plenty of reasons to perform "The Silencer," one of his favorite celebrations, during Miami's 27-game winning streak.

FEBRUARY 6, 2013: HEAT 114, HOUSTON 108

Another close game the whole way; James scored 32 points and Wade had 31 as the Heat survived.

FEBRUARY 8, 2013: HEAT 111, L.A. CLIPPERS 89

Miami outscored the Clippers 63–39 in the second and third quarters. James had 30 points and only needed 11 shots from the field to get there. Wade added 20, and Mario Chalmers had 18 for Miami.

FEBRUARY 10, 2013: HEAT 107, L.A. LAKERS 97

Tied at the half, the Heat got 32 points from James and 30 from Wade and pulled away in the final 24 minutes to top Kobe Bryant and the Lakers.

FEBRUARY 12, 2013: HEAT 117, PORTLAND 104

Bosh had 32 points to lead the victory. James remained red-hot, scoring 30 points, and Miami's streak reached six games. It was the sixth consecutive game in which James had 30 points on at least 60 percent shooting from the floor—an NBA first.

FEBRUARY 14, 2013: HEAT 110, OKLAHOMA CITY 100

Another masterpiece from James: 39 points, 12 rebounds, and seven assists. Bosh scored 20, and Wade and Ray Allen each scored 13 for Miami. The All-Star break came after this game.

FEBRUARY 20, 2013: HEAT 103, ATLANTA 90

The streak was in trouble going into the fourth, but Miami outscored Atlanta 40–17 in the final 12 minutes. James scored 24, Wade had 20, Shane Battier added 17, and Allen had 15.

FEBRUARY 21, 2013: HEAT 86, CHICAGO 67

The Bulls managed only 45 points in the final 36 minutes. James scored 26 for the Heat.

FEBRUARY 23, 2013: HEAT 114, PHILADELPHIA 90

Wade scored 33, and it was a triple-double for James—16 points, 11 assists, and 10 rebounds.

FEBRUARY 24, 2013: HEAT 109, CLEVELAND 105

The Heat led 68–46 early in the third quarter but trailed going into the fourth. Wade had 15 of his 24 points in the final quarter, and Miami survived to push the winning streak to 11 games.

FEBRUARY 26, 2013: HEAT 141, SACRAMENTO 129, DOUBLE OVERTIME

An amazing game. James scored 40, Wade scored 39, Allen scored 21 off the bench, and the Heat outscored the Kings 17–5 in overtime. James also had 16 assists and eight rebounds.

MARCH 1, 2013: HEAT 98, MEMPHIS 91

Wade scored 22 and

Dwyane Wade and the Miami Heat went 37–2 in their final 39 games of the 2012–13 regular season.

the Heat pulled away in the fourth quarter. James had 18 points, 10 assists, and eight rebounds. Battier scored 14, Bosh scored 13, and Allen had 10.

MARCH 3, 2013: HEAT 99, NEW YORK 93

Once again, the fourth quarter saved Miami. The Heat outscored the Knicks 26–16 in the fourth to erase a four-point deficit going into the final 12 minutes at Madison Square Garden. James scored 29, Wade had 20, Bosh had 16, and Battier was a perfect four-for-four from three-point range for 12 points.

MARCH 4, 2013: HEAT 97, MINNESOTA 81

The Heat set a franchise record with their 15th consecutive win. Notice a trend here? The fourth quarter was key: Heat 28, Timberwolves 18 was the score over the final 12 minutes. Wade finished with 32 points, James had 20, and Allen had 13.

MARCH 6, 2013: HEAT 97, ORLANDO 96

Miami scored the game's final four points to escape—Bosh made two free throws with 38 seconds left to cut Orlando's lead to one, and James won it on a layup with 3.2 seconds left. James scored 25, Wade had 24, and Bosh had 17 points and 10 rebounds.

MARCH 8, 2013: HEAT 102, PHILADELPHIA 93

The fourth quarter—again. Miami outscored the 76ers 26–18 in the final 12 minutes to win, with James scoring 25 points, Wade 22, and Bosh 16.

MARCH 10, 2013: HEAT 105, INDIANA 91

Chalmers played nearly a perfect game—seven for nine from the floor and seven for seven from the line, scoring a team-high 26. Bosh scored 24, Wade had 23, and James finished with 13 points, seven assists, and six rebounds.

MARCH 12, 2013: HEAT 98, ATLANTA 81

Finally, a bit of an easy one for Miami. Wade led a balanced Miami attack with 23 points, and the Heat led wire-to-wire as the winning streak hit 19 games.

Mario Chalmers and the Miami Heat had a slew of late-game comebacks during their 27-game winning streak.

MARCH 13, 2013: HEAT 98, PHILADELPHIA 94

The streak reached 20 games, and the Heat outscored the 76ers 7–3 in the final 72 seconds to get the win. Wade had four points in a span of 7.1 seconds late to put the game away. James scored 27 and Wade added 21.

MARCH 15, 2013: HEAT 107, MILWAUKEE 94

James and Bosh each scored 28, Wade added 20, and Miami held the Bucks to 15 second-quarter points. The winning streak went to 21 games.

MARCH 17, 2013: HEAT 108, TORONTO 91

Guess which quarter was pivotal? The fourth—again. Miami went back to where the streak started and kept it going, outscoring the Raptors 32–18 in the final quarter. Wade scored 24, James had 22, Allen had 20, and Bosh finished with 18.

MARCH 18, 2013: HEAT 105, BOSTON 103

Miami trailed by as many as 17 points in the first half. Many may remember this one for a spectacular dunk that James put down over Boston's Jason Terry—after which James got a technical for taunting on the play.

James scored with 10 seconds left to give Miami the lead for good. Paul Pierce missed a three-pointer that would have won it for Boston, and the Heat streak reached 23 games.

MARCH 20, 2013: HEAT 98, CLEVELAND 95

It almost ended on James's former home floor. Miami trailed 67–40 with 19 minutes left, then outscored Cleveland 58–28 the rest of the way. James had 25 points, 12 rebounds, and 10 assists. Chalmers scored 17, and the Heat survived.

MARCH 22, 2013: HEAT 103, DETROIT 89

Another rally, though not as pronounced: The Heat came back from an 11-point deficit this time. The streak hit 25 games after James went 12 for 15 from the floor and scored 29 points, Wade added 19, and Battier and Chalmers had 11 apiece.

MARCH 24, 2013: HEAT 109, CHARLOTTE 77

Down 11 in the early going again (OK, it was only 19–8, but still) the Heat ran away for consecutive win No. 26. James had 32 points, 10 assists, and eight rebounds, and he shot 11 of 14 from the floor and 10 of 11 from the foul line. Bosh and Norris Cole had 15 apiece, and the Heat didn't miss a beat by giving Wade a night off.

MARCH 25, 2013: HEAT 108, ORLANDO 94

Wade sat out again, and the Heat topped Orlando for the 27th and final win of the streak. James was a rebound shy of a triple-double after finishing with 24 points and 11 assists. Chalmers scored 17, while Bosh and Allen had 12 apiece and Rashard Lewis added 11 against his former club.

The streak would end two nights later, with Miami falling 101-97 in Chicago. No problem: The Heat would win 10 of their final 11 games of the regular season, meaning they went into the playoffs having won 37 out of their last 39 games.

Heat coach Erik Spoelstra (left) and team president Pat Riley (right) flank LeBron James as he accepts the 2013 NBA MVP award.

JAMES WINS NBA MVP AGAIN

THE NUMBERS: 26.8 points, 8.0 rebounds, 7.3 assists, and 1.7 steals per game to go with 56.5 percent shooting.

That was LeBron James in the 2012–13 season.

And he was rewarded with the MVP award again in one of the most one-sided votes in league history.

There were 121 first-place votes; James got 120 of them, with New York's Carmelo Anthony—who finished third—getting the other. Oklahoma City's Kevin Durant was second to James once again, matching the 1-2 order of finish from a year earlier.

James became the first player to win MVP and an NBA title in back-to-back seasons since Michael Jordan of the Chicago Bulls did it in 1991 and 1992. Before that, the most recent instance of simultaneous titles and MVP awards was when Bill Russell went back-to-back-to-back with the Boston Celtics in 1961, 1962, and 1963.

THE SAGA OF "BIRDMAN"

HOW HEAT FANS LOVED CHRIS ANDERSEN

THIS PLAYER, when he left the Miami Heat in February 2016, was 56th on the team's all-time list in scoring, along with 26th all-time in rebounding, 91st in assists . . . and probably first in tattoos.

He was Birdman.

If adoration from fans could be measured, Chris "Birdman" Andersen might be one of the Heat record-holders. He was colorful, literally and metaphorically. The tattoos that covered virtually every inch of his nearly 7-foot frame made him stand out, but his play was also valued by the Heat in their run to the 2013 NBA title.

Andersen had a tradition of sorts with Dr. Harlan Selesnick, the longtime Heat team physician. When Selesnick would see Andersen, the conversation would always go the same way.

Selesnick would ask how Andersen felt. Andersen would say he felt good. Selesnick would tell him he looked bad.

"And then he'd punch me," Selesnick said. It was all in good fun, like just about everything with Andersen in his Heat days.

"He was different than what his public persona was," Selesnick said. "Certainly, he was unique, but he was also very smart, very funny and a really good person. Just a really nice, caring person. People don't realize that."

Kids would show up at Heat games with their hair gelled into Mohawks, like his preferred haircut. Some kids even wore fake tattoos as well.

"I'm enjoying it, and being part of this team and this organization," Andersen said during that 2013 title run. "The guys in the locker room just made it so easy for me. To be a part of it is just special."

In 2001, Andersen became the first player ever called up to the NBA from what was then called the NBA Development League, now the G League.

Chris Andersen's one-of-a-kind style made him a fan favorite in Miami.

FOR MIKE MILLER, SHOOTING WAS AS EASY AS "ONE-SHOE-THREE"

THE BIGGEST shot of Game 6 of the 2013 NBA Finals? That's easy. That was Ray Allen's corner three-pointer with 5.2 seconds left that wound up forcing overtime, giving the Miami Heat renewed life and denied the San Antonio Spurs the NBA title.

But let's not forget one of the shots that made that comeback moment possible.

As Heat radio announcer Mike Inglis shrieked when Mike Miller made one of the shots of his life, "One! Shoe! Three!" Miller's left foot had popped out of his sneaker during a play on the defensive end, and he didn't have time to put the shoe back on since the game hadn't stopped.

So, with one sneaker on, he ran to the offensive end of the court. He cut across the court and was wide open on the right wing. LeBron James passed him the ball and Miller didn't hesitate before letting it fly from one of his favorite spots.

Swish.

No shoe. No problem. Miller's shot cut San Antonio's lead to 77–73, and those three points were pretty big – since the Heat needed every point they could muster in the comeback attempt that saved their season and ultimately sparked them to a second consecutive NBA title.

Mike Miller lets fly with a three-pointer in Game 6 of the 2013 NBA Finals against San Antonio, a few seconds after losing his shoe. He made the shot.

HEAT
13

BACARDI
DAKTRONICS
06.7
SPALDING
NBA TV
Finals
JAMES
6
BOSH
1
33

Miami's Ray Allen rises for one of the iconic shots in NBA history, a game-tying three-pointer that went through the net with 5.2 seconds left in Game 6 of the 2013 NBA Finals against San Antonio.

2013
JUNE 18

"REBOUND BOSH. BACK OUT TO ALLEN. *HIS THREE-POINTER. BANG!"*

RAY ALLEN had some unusual practice routines. Like the one where he would catch a ball while backtracking to the three-point line, knowing exactly how many steps it took to get there, then shooting the ball as quickly as he could.

Teammates would look on in disbelief. That would never happen in a game, they sometimes said.

Well . . .

Game 6, 2013 NBA Finals, Miami Heat vs. the San Antonio Spurs. The Spurs lead the series 3–2, lead the game 95–92, and are seconds away from winning the title. The Heat have the ball. LeBron James misses a three-pointer. Chris Bosh is under the basket, fighting for rebound position. And let's have broadcaster Mike Breen describe what happens next:

"Rebound Bosh. Back out to Allen. His three-pointer. BANG!"

With the yellow rope having already been brought out by NBA personnel to cordon the court for a trophy celebration, Allen made the shot of his life, the shot of Heat history. His stunning three-pointer with 5.2 seconds left sent Game 6 to overtime, and Bosh sealed the 103–100 win with a blocked shot in the final moments. Miami then prevailed in Game 7 for title No. 3 for the franchise, and a back-to-back for the Big Three.

"It was just incredible," Heat Managing General Partner Micky Arison said. "That's what it was. Incredible."

With Heat fan Jimmy Buffett (far left, white shirt, cap) looking on, Chris Bosh fights for a rebound in the final seconds of regulation of Game 6 of the 2013 NBA Finals.

NBA
GINOBILI
20
ALLEN
34

GAME 7, 2013 NBA FINALS, AND THE THIRD TITLE

RAY ALLEN'S shot that forced overtime in Game 6 of the 2013 NBA Finals saved the season and gave the Miami Heat one chance at back-to-back titles.

They did not waste the opportunity.

LeBron James finished off an MVP performance with 37 points and 12 rebounds, Dwyane Wade added 23 points, and the Heat beat the San Antonio Spurs 95–88 for the franchise's third championship and second in a row.

Also huge in Game 7: Shane Battier, who had 18 points, all on three-pointers. He also helped force Spurs star Tim Duncan into a pair of close-range misses in the final minute on shots that would have tied the game.

The Miami Heat celebrate the 2013 NBA title after beating the San Antonio Spurs in a seven-game championship series.

Allen and Chris Bosh, the heroes of Game 6, were a combined 0 for 9 from the field, but it didn't matter. Mario Chalmers made a three-pointer to close the third quarter for Miami, and the Heat led the rest of the way.

"My mindset is at a point where there is no relief," James said a few days after the series ended. "I love the burden. I love what I have to do for this team to win. If it happens and we get someone who relieves something from me as far as a big or a wing guy or something, then it'd be good for our team. But I'm not going up to those guys or approaching this summer saying 'I need help.' I'm coming back saying if we come back with this roster, we're going to compete for a championship."

He was right. A year later, the Heat were right back in the NBA Finals.

2013
JUNE 20

HOW DID WADE PLAY GAME 7 OF THE 2013 NBA FINALS? HE DOESN'T KNOW.

MIAMI HEAT guard Dwyane Wade's left knee was just about done going into Game 7 of the NBA Finals against the San Antonio Spurs in 2013.

The right knee wasn't much better, mind you.

The fact that Wade was out there at all was an absolute miracle: He had about a quart of fluid drained from one of his bad knees before Game 7. Wade played 39 minutes in the finale, scoring 23 points on 11 for 21 shooting as the Heat held off the Spurs 95–88. It was Miami's second consecutive championship and the third of Wade's Heat career.

"I went through a lot," Wade said when it was all over. "But I'm at peace now."

He needed platelet-rich plasma therapy late in the regular season to help him deal with three bone bruises around his right knee, including one directly under the kneecap. An MRI exam ruled out other issues during the Eastern Conference finals against Indiana, but Wade was ready to tell Heat coach Erik Spoelstra that he needed to play limited minutes.

It was like Spoelstra knew what Wade was thinking. So, a preemptive strike was taken. Spoelstra surprised Wade by telling him he wanted him more—not less—involved in the game plan.

It worked out. He scored 21 points in the East finals finale against the Pacers and a combined 57 points—looking very much like his best self—in Games 4 and 5 of the NBA Finals against the Spurs.

But early in Game 6 of that series with San Antonio, Wade banged into the Spurs' Manu Ginobili. Wade's left knee, he said, swelled to the size of a coconut.

He needed treatment during Game 6, then had hours and hours of treatment going into Game 7.

"Some players probably wouldn't have played," Spoelstra said.

Miami's Dwyane Wade, shooting over San Antonio's Tim Duncan, played through serious knee discomfort in the 2013 NBA Finals.

JAMES WINS NBA FINALS MVP, AGAIN

THERE WAS no shortage of heroes for the Miami Heat in the 2013 NBA Finals against the San Antonio Spurs.

There was Ray Allen, for the season-saving three-pointer with 5.2 seconds left in regulation of Game 6 when the Spurs were closing in on the title. There was Chris Bosh, who got the offensive rebound to extend that play—and got the assist by finding Allen with the pass that set up that shot as well. There was Dwyane Wade, who played in that series with his knees aching.

And, of course, there was LeBron James. For the second consecutive season, he was the MVP, a champion, and the NBA Finals MVP as well.

James averaged 25.3 points in that series, 31.8 points over the final four games of the matchup. He saved his best for last: 33 points in Game 4, 25 in Game 5, 32 in Game 6, and 37 in Game 7—while playing virtually the entire way in those four contests.

He also had two triple-doubles in the series, with 18 points, 18 rebounds, and 10 assists in Game 1, then 32 points, 10 rebounds, and 11 assists in Game 6.

LeBron James (center) celebrates the 2013 NBA Finals win inside the joyous Miami Heat locker room.

2013
DECEMBER

A CHRISTMAS PARTY TO REMEMBER

THE MIAMI Heat Christmas party is a big deal, especially to hosts Pat and Chris Riley. They plan it for weeks, and guests—usually players, coaches, and some of the staff—all take part in a gift exchange where there is a spending limit.

We think Dwyane Wade didn't play by the rules in 2013.

Technically, the big gift he gave that year wasn't at the Heat Christmas party. But that night, he offered up another gift of sorts; he asked actress Gabrielle Union to marry him.

"She said YES!!!" Wade posted to his accounts on what was then called Twitter along with Instagram. For proof, he also posted a photo of Union wearing a large diamond solitaire on the ring finger of her left hand.

"A special evening," Heat Managing General Partner Micky Arison wrote on social media that night.

Wade proposed to Union before the party. Everybody knew it was coming, especially since the couple's Christmas cards that year were sent with a return address sticker calling them the "Wade-Union Family."

"The MiamiHEAT Christmas party always brings great traditions and the BEST surprises," Adrienne Bosh, Chris Bosh's wife, posted on social media that night.

For the record, the real gift Wade gave to teammates that season—at least those who was part of Miami's second consecutive run to an NBA championship a few months earlier—was green jackets, similar to the ones presented to the winners of the Masters tournament at Augusta National Golf Club.

2014
JANUARY 14

THE HEAT RETURN TO THE WHITE HOUSE

PRESIDENT BARACK Obama is from Chicago. He is a Chicago Bulls fan. He is not a Miami Heat fan.

But when the Heat came back to the White House for a second consecutive year in 2014—this time to celebrate winning the 2013 NBA title—Obama said he found some parallels between being president and being the best team in basketball.

"I want to congratulate Coach (Erik) Spoelstra for the outstanding work that he does; legendary team President, Pat Riley, for his outstanding leadership; and all the coaches and players, members of the staff and crew to make a championship season," Obama said. "This group has won twice now, but it's gone to the finals three times. And sometimes it feels like they're still fighting for

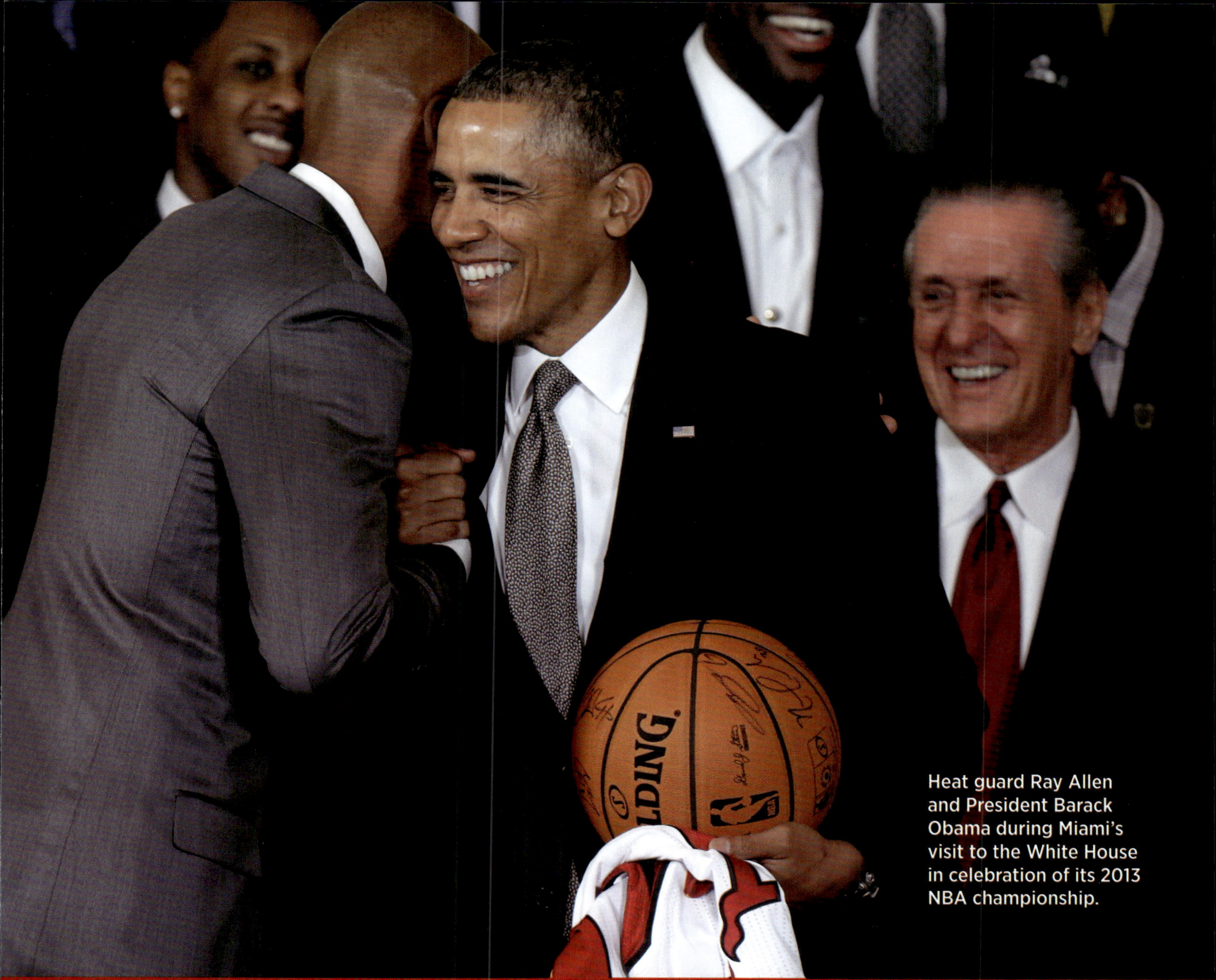

Heat guard Ray Allen and President Barack Obama during Miami's visit to the White House in celebration of its 2013 NBA championship.

a little respect. I can relate to that," Obama said, as the room broke into laughter.

Obama kept the room in hysterics. He poked fun at Chris Andersen and his mohawk haircut and tattoos. He lauded Ray Allen for the three-pointer that saved the Heat in Game 6 of the finals against San Antonio, then teased him about the off-color language he used after making that shot (and how Allen, uh, suggested that workers take the yellow rope away from the floor since the trophy ceremony wouldn't be happening). And he even knew that Mario Chalmers, a major part of the 2012 and 2013 title teams, tended to get yelled at by teammates from time to time.

"I think we should take a picture, but we should make it quick before one of these guys starts yelling at Mario," Obama said to loud laughter. "I mean, sometimes it's just a bad pass, guys. It's not Mario's fault."

And with that, he turned toward Chalmers. "I got your back, man," the leader of the free world told the Heat point guard.

LeBron James, in a mask, scored a team-record 61 points for the Miami Heat during a game in 2014.

JAMES, IN A MASK, SCORES 61

LEBRON JAMES'S status on March 3, 2014, was in a bit of question for the Miami Heat. He was about 10 days removed from getting his nose broken by Serge Ibaka in a game against Oklahoma City. There were a few weeks left in the season. Miami's playoff spot was already secured. It might have been a good spot for a night off.

Instead, it became a night to make Heat history. A masked man that night, James scored a team-record 61 points in a dazzling display in what became a 124–107 win over the Charlotte Bobcats.

He was 22 of 33 from the field, 14 of 23 on two-pointers, eight of 10 on three-pointers (some of them several feet behind the arc), and nine of 12 from the foul line, and he added seven rebounds.

By quarters, James had 11 in the first, 13 more in the second, 25 in the third (going 5 of 5 from deep, making him 8 of 8 on the night to that point), and then capped the performance with 12 more in the fourth.

The 61 points broke a record that had stood for nearly 19 years, that being Glen Rice's 56-point effort for the Heat on April 15, 1995, against Orlando. And the 61 points was also a career-best for James, the NBA's all-time scoring king.

THE BIG THREE ERA ENDS WITH A LOSS IN SAN ANTONIO

IT ENDED quietly, almost as if those involved knew the era had run its course. A chapter ended for the Miami Heat with a loss to San Antonio in the 2014 NBA Finals.

Miami lost to San Antonio in five games. The rematch of the title series from the year before went the Spurs' way this time. And just like that, though nobody knew it for absolute certain at the time, the Big Three era was over.

James was leaving. He made it official a few weeks later, announcing that he was going back to Cleveland after his four years in Miami. He went back to the Cavaliers determined to make good on his promise of bringing a championship to northeast Ohio, and in 2016, he would do just that.

Ray Allen, Shane Battier, and Rashard Lewis all played their final games as well. It was over after two championships, four Eastern Conference championships, and four trips to the NBA Finals.

"We didn't know what to expect when we decided to become teammates," Heat guard Dwyane Wade would say when those 2014 Finals ended. "We have no reason not to be proud of each other for what we've accomplished on and off the court for these four years together."

A somber Dwyane Wade and LeBron James during the 2014 NBA Finals loss to the San Antonio Spurs. It would be James's last series as a member of the Heat.

THE BIG THREE ERA BY THE NUMBERS

SOME WILL say that the four-year run that Dwyane Wade, LeBron James, and Chris Bosh had with the Miami Heat wasn't a total success. After all, they lost in the NBA Finals twice and won "only" two championships, the naysayers said when it was all over.

They have a case, of course.

The numbers also make a strong case for how good that run was.

Over those four years, the Heat had 283 wins, including playoffs. That was the most in the NBA over that span and 61 more than any other team in the Eastern Conference. They made four consecutive trips to the NBA Finals. They won NBA titles in 2012 and 2013.

Now, dig deeper. It was a business boom for the Heat; every home game at AmericanAirlines Arena sold out in that span, and Miami was at or near the top of the merchandise-sold list by the metrics that the NBA uses to track such things. The Heat won 27 consecutive games in one stretch during that Big Three era, the second-longest winning streak in NBA history. There were two other 12-game winning streaks in there as well. Wade, James, and Bosh were All-Stars in each of those four seasons. James won the NBA MVP award twice—becoming the first Heat player to capture that trophy. Globally, the Heat became a major brand.

"We decided to come together all for one goal—to win championships and we succeeded," Wade said. "We were friends when we first joined the league and created an unbreakable bond."

LeBron James, Dwyane Wade, and Chris Bosh went to four NBA Finals in their four seasons together with the Miami Heat.

Shane Battier of the Miami Heat helps at a charity event inside the team's arena. Battier was honored by the NBA for his service to teammates and the community.

SHANE BATTIER WINS TWYMAN-STOKES TEAMMATE OF THE YEAR

SHANE BATTIER was a college great at Duke, an NBA champion with the Miami Heat, and a success on and off the court. By 2014, his career was already storied, his place in basketball lore secured.

And then he got something he called one of the biggest honors of his basketball life.

Battier was the 2014 winner of the NBA's Twyman-Stokes Teammate of the Year award, which recognizes selfless play, leadership, work as a role model to other players, and commitment.

The NBA made a $25,000 donation to the Battier Take Charge Foundation, which raised money to help provide children with educational and leadership opportunities.

"Although the guys in the locker room couldn't cast any votes for me, I'd like to think they would've voted for me if they could," Battier said. "I hope they know that I love them and I appreciate them and everything I do I try to make that locker room better and this team better."

Battier had been up for the award several times in his career, then finally won it.

"I think everybody would agree that you could make a case for a lot of guys in the locker room, but Shane, he's the ultimate teammate," Heat coach Erik Spoelstra said. "Selfless. He'll do whatever it takes. He's a leader. He's playing for his brothers, his teammates, and you can feel it. So it's a great award."

The award honors Basketball Hall of Famers Jack Twyman and Maurice Stokes, who were linked by an incident that happened in the final game of the 1957–58 regular season. Stokes suffered a brain injury and was paralyzed. Twyman supported him for the remainder of his life, eventually even serving as his legal guardian and advocate.

Battier called the story of Twyman and Stokes "an amazing story of brotherhood." That's what teammates felt they got every day from Battier.

"There's no better guy out there than Shane," Heat captain Udonis Haslem said at the time.

THE GREATNESS OF ALONZO MOURNING

When the Miami Heat began retiring jerseys of franchise greats, team president Pat Riley insisted that one person had to be the first.

That person was Alonzo Mourning. "There's only one Zo," Riley said.

He averaged 17.1 points and 8.5 rebounds in his NBA career, one that spanned 16 seasons with Miami, Charlotte, and New Jersey. Mourning was a seven-time All-Star, a two-time defensive player of the year, and an Olympic gold medalist. He had his No. 33 jersey retired by the Heat in a star-studded ceremony that went much longer than planned during halftime of a game against Orlando in 2009.

"He had to be the first one to have his jersey retired by this franchise," Riley said at the time. "He earned that, many times over."

Mourning spent the bulk of his playing years with Miami, and he never really left. After his playing days were done he went into the Heat front office with the title of Vice President of Player Programs—helping to oversee, the team said, "the personal and professional development of Heat players, while providing direct support and one-on-one mentoring." He was a regular at Heat practices and games, almost always in sharply pressed button-down shirts and dress slacks. And in August 2014, he went into the Basketball Hall of Fame.

But Mourning's story is more about the journey than any statistic or award.

He was raised by a foster mother who took him and 48 other kids into her home. From there, Mourning became a star at Georgetown, then an NBA icon who couldn't even be derailed by a kidney disease that necessitated a transplant while still in the prime of his career, and finally, a champion with the Heat.

"You don't think about going to the Hall of Fame. It's your reward," Mourning said. "This was the last thing on my mind. I had an amazing career. The journey was spectacular for me, personally. If no one else saw it that way, then so be it."

John Thompson, his coach at Georgetown, and Riley are two of the people who Mourning credits most for showing him how to win on and off the court. The other is Fannie Threet, the foster mother who died at the age of 98 and the person who Mourning speaks of with more reverence than anyone else. And when the Hall of Fame called, it meant the world to Mourning.

"It's the pinnacle of the sport," Mourning said. "And outside of the birth of my children and winning a championship, it's the pinnacle of it all."

Alonzo Mourning is still considered one of the best leaders and players in Miami Heat history.

JAMES RETURNS FOR THE FIRST TIME AFTER LEAVING

ON CHRISTMAS Eve 2014, LeBron James and Dwyane Wade hung out together to celebrate the holiday. It was like old times, like the four years they spent as Miami Heat teammates.

On Christmas Day 2014, they went head-to-head again.

The NBA schedule-makers knew what they were doing when putting the 2014–15 schedule together. James's first trip back to Miami that season, his first after a four-year, four-Eastern-Conference-titles, two-NBA-championships run with the Heat, just happened to be when the Cleveland Cavaliers visited on December 25.

James got a standing ovation from most in the crowd when a video tribute was played during a first-quarter stoppage of the game, and he seemed deeply moved by both the images, the memories, and the reaction. Wade scored 24 of his 31 points in the first half, Luol Deng added 25 points for Miami, and the Heat won 101-91.

"We played against each other for seven years, man. The weirdness just wasn't there. It wasn't like we played against each other our whole career and the breakup happened," Wade said afterward. "We played against each other for seven years, then with each other for a period of time, then he went back to the same situation and I'm in the same place."

James embraced Wade before and after the game and shared plenty of greetings with people in Miami that he knew and worked with during his four-year run with the Heat.

"We're going to go about our business and do what we need to do in our profession," James said. "You'll never let friendship come in between that."

Cleveland's LeBron James smiles at Miami's Dwyane Wade during the game between their teams on Christmas 2014.

SHAQ'S NO. 32 GOES TO THE RAFTERS

SHAQUILLE O'NEAL honestly never thought the Miami Heat would retire his jersey.

Yes, he arrived amid great fanfare in 2004 and helped deliver the franchise's first NBA championship two years later. He also basically forced his way out of Miami two years after that, getting traded in 2008 and not ending his tenure on the best of terms with Heat officials.

Which is why he did not expect the Heat to ever call with good news.

"This is an inside joke for all the Miami people," O'Neal said on the night of December 22, 2016, when his jersey went to the rafters—just the third at that time in team history behind Alonzo Mourning and Tim Hardaway. "It's definitely unexpected."

Truth be told, the Heat always knew his jersey would be retired. It was simply a question of when.

"He's a once-in-a-lifetime player," Heat President Pat Riley said. "There are a lot of them in the history of the NBA, but he's a once-in-a-lifetime acquisition for us and meant so much to us."

Later, Riley added perhaps the simplest reason why O'Neal was honored. "We would not have won the championship in 2006 without the efforts of Shaquille O'Neal," Riley said.

Shaquille O'Neal's jersey banner hangs above the court in Miami after the ceremony when it was officially retired in 2016.

BAM ADEBAYO DRAFTED BY THE HEAT

THE MIAMI Heat didn't take Bam Adebayo with the 14th overall pick in the 2017 NBA Draft because he, like team President Pat Riley, went to Kentucky.

They took Adebayo because they knew what he could become.

Adebayo joined the Heat after just one year playing for John Calipari at Kentucky, and there were instant comparisons to Alonzo Mourning in Miami. Fast-forward eight years, and Adebayo is already one of the Heat all-time-great big men and the franchise record-holder in double-doubles. He's closing in on Udonis Haslem's team rebounding record, and he serves as the Heat captain.

And Adebayo told the world why all that would happen on his draft night.

"I bring athleticism. I bring defense. I bring energy," he said.

All of that was true, as it turned out. And Adebayo had a hunch going into the draft that Miami would be the one to call his name.

"You know, when I went to work out, I spoke to Pat Riley," Adebayo said on draft night. "They seem real cool. They seemed really interested in me, and I seemed real interested in them. I bring a smile to everybody, and I bring a lot of energy."

Years later, it can be confirmed: Those details still hold true.

NBA Commissioner Adam Silver greets Miami's Bam Adebayo at the 2017 NBA draft.

THE WEIRDEST SEASON IN HEAT HISTORY

FIRST 11-30, THEN 30-11

SAY THIS much for the 2016–17 Miami Heat season: It was unlike any other.

The first half was really, really bad.

The second half was really, really good.

Miami went 11–30 in the season's first 41 games, flirting with the worst record in the NBA at that point. Dwyane Wade was gone, having gone to Chicago for what he thought was a better deal. Chris Bosh was sidelined by blood clots for the entire season. Justise Winslow missed most of the season. The Heat lost more players for more games to injury and illness than any other team in the NBA that season.

And then, in an instant, it all changed.

The Heat went 30–11 in the final 41 games of the season, missing the playoffs in a tiebreaker. They won 13 straight games at one point, knocking off eventual NBA champion Golden State at home—on a basket in the final second by Dion Waiters—to highlight that streak. They beat then-reigning NBA champion Cleveland three times in four meetings. There was clearly something there that worked.

It all came down to the final night of the season. The Heat won, but they didn't get the help they needed and they missed the playoffs.

This is where things got odd. Most of the players stuck around in Miami long after the season, working out together on a regular basis all the way into June. That doesn't happen in the NBA. When a season ends, players scatter. Not this team.

"You look at everything we went through, and there's only one thing you can say," Heat Captain Udonis Haslem said. "We had a hell of a season."

Erik Spoelstra was voted the NBA's co-coach of the year by his peers in the National Basketball Coaches Association. Hassan Whiteside won the league's rebounding title. The Heat became the first team in NBA history to be 19 games under .500 at any point in the season and still win at least 41 games.

But the playoffs weren't meant to be.

"I don't know if I've ever wanted something more for a team," Spoelstra said.

Dion Waiters shoots what became the game-winner in Miami's victory over eventual NBA champion Golden State during the 2016-17 season.

#MSDSTRONG

THE HEAT REACT TO TRAGEDY

THEY CALLED him Guac. His name was Joaquin Oliver. He was a 17-year-old student at Marjory Stoneman Douglas High School in Parkland, Florida, about 45 miles or so north of Miami. He loved the Miami Heat. He loved Dwyane Wade.

So, when Wade returned to the Heat after time with the Cleveland Cavaliers in February 2018, Oliver was overjoyed.

And a few days later, he was gone. Oliver was one of the 17 people, mostly students, killed in a shooting massacre at the school on February 14, 2018. His family would bury him in a Wade jersey.

Maybe it was a coincidence. Maybe it was more. But Wade's best game to that point that season came on a night where he scrawled Oliver's name on his sneakers. Wade scored a season-high 27 points and connected on the game-winning basket to lift Miami over the Philadelphia 76ers, 102–101 on February 27, 2018.

He couldn't believe Oliver's family included him when it was time to lay Guac to rest.

"That they thought of me in that process, as something that he would have wanted, is mindboggling," Wade said.

Dwyane Wade stands for the national anthem with Andrea Ghersi, the sister of slain Marjory Stoneman Douglas student Joaquin "Guac" Oliver.

Heat guard Dwyane Wade greets Miami Heat President Pat Riley at All-Star weekend in 2019.

WADE'S FINAL ALL-STAR GAME

MIAMI HEAT guard Dwyane Wade got to Charlotte, North Carolina, for the start of All-Star weekend in 2019—his final All-Star weekend as a player—and thought the agenda for his first night in town was just a dinner with close friends and family.

He'd been lied to.

There were hundreds of people at this dinner, one that had been a closely kept secret for weeks. For hours, wine flowed—Wade, seated on a throne, had two glasses going at one point during the evening. And stories also flowed. The food, sea bass and filet mignon, was fabulous. But the tributes were even better.

Among the speakers: Caron Butler, Donovan Mitchell, Isiah Thomas, Tim Hardaway, Charles Barkley, Chris Paul, Carmelo Anthony, and Heat President Pat Riley.

"No one—when I say no one, I mean no one—has done the things at a professional level out of Chicago on a basketball stage better than Dwyane Wade," said Thomas, who always had an affinity for Wade because they both hail from the Chicago area.

Magic Johnson was there, too. He lauded Wade for being a leader, an ambassador for the game, and a champion.

"We're going to miss him," Johnson said.

In the end, Wade ended up loving the surprise.

"A perfect night," he said.

WADE, TO BEAT THE WARRIORS

DWYANE WADE would eventually call it "the ugliest shot" of his life.

But it is forever part of Miami Heat lore.

It was in Wade's final season, the Heat trailing Golden State—then the best team in the NBA—by two points with about 10 seconds remaining. Wade brings the ball upcourt, with Kevin Durant waiting to guard him. An epic battle was coming. Everybody in the building knew it.

Wade tried to get past Durant, to no avail. He felt like any shot he took would be denied, so he passed the ball to Dion Waiters and expected him to take the last shot. So, apparently, did the Warriors—who double-teamed Waiters right away.

Waiters gives the ball back to Wade. And years later, here's how he explained what happened next:

"I shoot. It gets blocked. The rebound just falls back into my hands. I just heave it up toward the rim and hope a prayer gets answered."

It got answered.

Wade's shot hit the backboard and fell through the net, giving the Heat a one-point win at the buzzer. Wade took a victory lap and jumped onto the scorer's table, one of his signature moves at such times.

"To me, that play is a metaphor for everything in my life," Wade said years later. "The chips were down and we overcame the odds. The play fell apart and we found a way to make something happen anyway. We kept playing hard, all the way to the end."

Dwyane Wade leaps onto a courtside table after a game-winning shot against the Golden State Warriors in 2019.

2019
MARCH 26

BOSH GETS HIS JERSEY RETIRED

SAY THIS for Chris Bosh: He knew how to rebound.

There were the obvious ways, of course, like getting a season-saving, championship-saving rebound in Game 6 of the 2013 NBA Finals to set up Ray Allen's game-tying shot for the Miami Heat with 5.2 seconds left against the San Antonio Spurs.

There were also the not-so-obvious ways, like bouncing back from terrible luck when it came to his health and how that took years off his career.

It took some time, but Bosh made peace with the way that blood clots ended his NBA career without warning and when he was still in his prime. The Heat retired his No. 1 jersey in 2019; Bosh's was the fourth to go to the rafters, after Alonzo Mourning, Tim Hardaway, and Shaquille O'Neal. (Dwyane Wade's and Udonis Haslem's would follow, and the Heat have already said LeBron James's will go there one day as well.)

"It's very awesome," Bosh said. "I thought I had more time, but in the time I gave it was still worthy enough to have the organization and the great Pat Riley consider this. Pretty cool."

Bosh played 13 seasons, six in Miami after seven in Toronto. He averaged 19.2 points and 8.5 rebounds, was an All-Star 11 times, and won two championships. And he went to the Basketball Hall of Fame, first as a player, then again in 2025 as part of the 2008 US Olympic men's basketball "Redeem Team."

He was known to have dealt with clots twice in his Heat career, and the second chapter led the team to say that he couldn't risk playing again. Bosh clashed with the team about that, and they found themselves at odds over the issue for a year or two. But the Heat didn't blink, saying they would not let Bosh risk his health.

In time, they made up. Bosh understood Miami's decision. And he made peace with it.

"I'm very happy with where I'm at, with how I feel," Bosh said. "That's what is most important. I couldn't even imagine trying to play basketball again. So I had a pretty solid run. And yeah, it's over. But it was a pretty solid run."

Chris Bosh watches his Heat jersey get raised to the rafters during a ceremony in 2019.

WADE'S CAREER

ONE UNLIKE ANY OTHER

IT WAS clear when Dwyane Wade retired that his name would hang on a banner, and that No. 3 would sway from the rafters of AmericanAirlines Arena sometime in the next few months. (The arena changed names, but you get the idea.)

It was also clear that he'd get a statue. It's now outside the arena.

And it was clear that he'd get a stretch of Biscayne Boulevard named for him, too. That also happened; you can drive along Dwyane Wade Boulevard these days.

Because he put his stamp on everything, it seems like his name is on everything. That goes back to 2010, when Miami-Dade County—this is true—renamed itself Miami-Wade County for a week during that wild free agent summer. The name reverted on paper, but people still call it Wade County.

"I appreciate all of it," Wade said. "But . . . "

His voice trailed off. He knows none of it was necessary. Let's face it: the Heat won't have another Dwyane Wade.

The game-winner in Game 1 of the playoffs in 2004 over Baron Davis. His first playoff game. Who does that? Dwyane Wade does that. And if anyone thought what happened that night was a fluke, the next 15 years proved them wrong.

He wasn't from Miami. But by the end, he was officially a son of Miami.

"And that's a forever thing," Heat President Pat Riley said.

Dwyane Wade retired as Miami's all-time leading scorer, a record that nobody has come close to approaching.

TYLER HERRO DRAFTED BY THE HEAT

THE MIAMI Heat drafted a Kentucky player in Round 1 in 2017, then didn't have a pick the following season.

So, in 2019, when the Heat had a first-rounder again—they looked once more to Kentucky.

Tyler Herro was the No. 13 pick in the 2019 draft, taken by the Heat one spot ahead of where they had landed Bam Adebayo two years earlier. And like Adebayo, Herro was well-versed in the history of Pat Riley and what it meant for another Kentucky player to head to Miami.

"He's a former Kentucky guy," Herro said of Riley, who played for Adolph Rupp at Kentucky in the 1960s. "Obviously he has a great tradition in Miami. What they've done, they've won a lot of games and a lot of series and championships."

Herro was asked if he had met Riley.

"Yes, sir," he said.

And did Riley make him nervous?

"No, sir," he said.

Herro came to the Heat after growing up and playing his high school basketball in Wisconsin, where the winters are, let's say, a bit harsher than in balmy, tropical South Florida.

He was asked on draft night what excited him the most.

"Probably the warm weather," Herro said. "Finally get to spend some winters where it's not too cold. I'm just excited to get to Miami and get started."

Tyler Herro poses on his draft night in 2019 after being selected by the Miami Heat.

TRAE YOUNG CALLED GAME.

HE WAS RIGHT, SORT OF.

SOMETIMES, FANS leave games early. They want to beat the traffic. The game is decided. They've got an early morning. There are all sorts of reasons.

If they were among the 19,600 fans at the Miami Heat vs. Atlanta Hawks game on December 10, 2019, you would hope they didn't leave early. They would have missed a finish like few others.

Atlanta scored for a six-point lead with 59 seconds left in regulation, the Heat called time-out, and as he was walking to the bench Hawks star Trae Young yelled "It's over" to the Miami crowd.

Well, he was right.

Miami scored the next 22 points. The Heat scored the final six points of regulation, and then they scored the first 16 points of overtime, earning them a 135–121 victory on a night loaded with stats.

Duncan Robinson tied a franchise record with 10 three-pointers. Jimmy Butler and Bam Adebayo each had triple-doubles. Kendrick Nunn scored a career-high 36 points, one off the Heat rookie single-game record. Robinson scored 34, a career high. Adebayo finished with a career-high 30 points, 11 rebounds, and 11 assists. Butler had 20 points, a career-high 18 rebounds, and 10 assists.

"I don't think anybody really thought the Heat were relevant," Adebayo said. "We're making people watch us."

Heat center Bam Adebayo talks to teammates before a game in the 2019–20 season.

Heat star Jimmy Butler poses inside the NBA's pandemic bubble at Walt Disney World in Lake Buena Vista, Florida, in 2020.

FOR JIMMY BUTLER, COFFEE WAS AN OBSESSION

AND A CAREER

THIS ALL started in the bubble during the 2020 pandemic restart at Walt Disney World in Lake Buena Vista, Florida. Jimmy Butler would make coffee. And he would charge $20 a cup for it.

NBA players—pardon the pun—poured in to see what all the fuss was about. Butler insists nobody, not even teammates, got anything for free.

That was the beginning of BigFace Coffee.

Over the next few years he sold merchandise, opened a coffee shop in Miami, and detailed how he would routinely drink 10 cappuccinos a day. And he was serious about it, to the point that he would make field trips to faraway lands to study how coffee is grown and harvested.

"As much as the offer was appealing to me, he still was a potential enemy, so I didn't want to go there," Los Angeles Lakers coach Frank Vogel said during that season's NBA Finals, when his team faced Butler and the Heat. "But $20 is a lot for a cup of coffee. I don't know if I would have spent that much, anyway."

Butler's bubble coffee rules were simple: Cash only, exact change required. Someone tried to pay with a $100 bill. Change was not offered. Butler had tough rules. He somehow got away with it.

"I give Jimmy a lot of credit," former Heat teammate Goran Dragic said in 2022. "He said he was going to learn everything he could about coffee and he meant it."

The funny thing is that Butler hated coffee when he first tried it. He was traded from Miami to Golden State in 2025—but said his store in Miami will remain in place, with plans to add more in California.

"This is a very real thing for me," Butler said.

2020
SEPTEMBER

ADEBAYO WITH THE BLOCK, AND IT BECAME A MOMENT

IT'S THE 2020 Eastern Conference Finals, inside the NBA bubble at Lake Buena Vista, Florida. The Miami Heat against the Boston Celtics.

Miami is up by two with about three seconds left in overtime. Jayson Tatum has a dunk that would tie the game.

That's when Bam Adebayo happened.

Adebayo somehow got his hand between the ball and the rim, pinning it against Tatum's own hand for a block that essentially was the capper of Miami's Game 1 win of that series. The Heat would go on to win the series and make the NBA Finals.

The block was the story of the bubble for a day or two. Adebayo couldn't believe that he was the subject of a tweet from Basketball Hall of Famer Magic Johnson, who called the block "the best defensive play I've seen ever in the playoffs!!!!"

Heat President Pat Riley promised Adebayo that the block would be prominently displayed in photos at the team's arena in Miami—Riley delivered on that promise—and Dwyane Wade texted Adebayo to tell him how impressed he was with the play.

"I had to watch it again and again to almost like just capture how special of a play it was," Heat guard Duncan Robinson said.

Miami's Bam Adebayo blocks a dunk attempt by Boston's Jayson Tatum in Game 1 of the 2020 NBA Eastern Conference Finals.

Mickey Mouse is among the "fans" shown on a digital screen during the 2020 NBA playoffs at Walt Disney World in Lake Buena Vista, Florida.

THE BUBBLE. AND A FINALS RUN.

SOME ARENAS have nicknames in the NBA. Madison Square Garden is simply "The Garden" or "MSG." For years, AmericanAirlines Arena in Miami was known to everybody in South Florida as "the Triple-A," and let's be honest, there are people who still call it that even though the name has changed a few times.

Which brings us to Walt Disney World in Lake Buena Vista, Florida.

It was The Bubble.

It saved the 2019–20 NBA season, the one that was halted on March 11, 2020 when Rudy Gobert, then of the Utah Jazz, tested positive for COVID-19. In the end, 22 of the league's 30 teams moved into the bubble in July to finish the season under strict rules and without fans in the seats. (Some were shown from remote locations on digital screens surrounding the court.) Testing took place daily. The outside world was kept outside. It was not easy.

But it worked. The season was saved. And the Miami Heat made their way to the NBA Finals, the Bubble Finals as some called them.

"I wanted everybody to have perspective on how difficult this is, how extraordinary of an experience all of this is," Miami coach Erik Spoelstra said. "Being part of this bubble, being here for 80-plus days, surviving all of it and earning the right to compete for an NBA title."

It also became a platform to talk about change in society.

The league put the words "Black Lives Matter" on the courts. Jerseys were modified to allow for social messages. Players almost shut the bubble down because they felt not enough people cared about demands for racial equality on the outside.

"Statements were made," Heat center Bam Adebayo said. "It wasn't just basketball. It was a lot more than basketball."

GORAN DRAGIC

A SON OF SLOVENIA FINDS A HOME IN MIAMI

GORAN DRAGIC played for a lot of teams during his NBA career. But he became an All-Star with the Miami Heat.

And his time in Miami defined his NBA years.

His lone All-Star appearance was as a member of the Heat, and he was beloved in South Florida as his career was winding down. After he retired Miami remained his home, and he was a regular at Heat games for the first couple years after his playing days ended.

Dragic was beloved in Miami. The Heat even put up billboards in Slovenia when Dragic became a free agent in 2020, saying things like "Your second family is always with you." As soon as Dragic saw that, his mind was made up. He'd re-sign with Miami.

He helped Miami reach the 2020 NBA Finals, played in The Bubble at Walt Disney World in Lake Buena Vista, Florida, because of the COVID-19 pandemic. Dragic hurt his foot early in that series and appeared in only two games. That doomed Miami's chances at a title.

"Can you do something for me?" he asked a reporter when that series against the Los Angeles Lakers ended, the Heat having lost in six games. "Tell the fans we really tried and I'm sorry. I really tried."

Goran Dragic (left) celebrating a play with fellow Heat guard Tyler Herro.

Udonis Haslem (left) walks with Miami-Dade County Mayor Daniella Levine Cava to a memorial site honoring those lost in the Champlain Towers collapse near Miami in 2021.

BIGGER THAN BASKETBALL

IN MIAMI, THE HEAT STEP UP

JUNE 2021 was a time of unspeakable tragedy in the Miami area.

It also was a reminder of what the Miami Heat mean to the community. "We have to be more than a basketball team," said Steve Stowe, a longtime Heat executive who, among other things, helps with team outreach.

The middle-of-the-night collapse of the Champlain Towers South building killed 98 people and was one of the deadliest disasters of its kind in US history. It was also another example of the Heat going into the community where it was needed to help South Florida get through tragedy.

Miami native Udonis Haslem visited the site about a week after the incident, with one arm draped over the shoulders of Miami-Dade County Mayor Daniella Levine Cava as they walked slowly through the memorial scene set up near the spot where the tower once stood. It was a rare instance of the Heat captain being at a loss for words.

"Continue to pray," he said.

Haslem visited with first responders, who had been working around the clock for about a week at the time of his visit. He laid a wreath of red and white flowers at the fence of the property, and added his thoughts to a memorial banner at the site.

"We're so grateful for a towering man to come and show his love and support," Levine Cava said, while flanked by the 6-foot-8 Haslem.

2021
OCTOBER

ADEBAYO
OLYMPIC GOLD MEDALIST (PART 1)

THEY HANG banners for championships in Miami. The three NBA championships, the Eastern Conference championships, even smaller banners for division championships (with multiple years on each banner).

They also have them for retired numbers; the current list includes Alonzo Mourning, Tim Hardaway, Shaquille O'Neal, Dwyane Wade, Chris Bosh, and Udonis Haslem. LeBron James is certain to be there one day as well; the Heat have already said that will be happening.

It's entirely possible that Bam Adebayo's No. 13 goes to the rafters one day. But in 2021, Adebayo set out for a different banner.

Somewhere along the way the Heat decided to pay tribute to Olympic gold medalists who won those medals while playing for Miami. (It doesn't apply to Heat players who won them when they were with another franchise, which is why the golds won by Kevin Love, Jimmy Butler, Kyle Lowry, and others haven't gotten the same treatment.) But win Olympic gold while you play for the Heat, and you get a banner for that accomplishment.

Adebayo knew this when he went to the Tokyo Games that were scheduled for 2020 and wound up getting played in 2021 because of the delay caused by the COVID-19 pandemic.

It was foremost on his mind after the Americans beat France in the gold-medal game in Tokyo. Still draped in the American flag that he had on the court at the end of that game, Adebayo was screaming when he trotted off the court and into the media area that he had to pass through on his way to the Team USA locker room.

"Give me my banner! Give me my . . . banner!" Adebayo shouted, at no one in particular.

It was, indeed, a banner accomplishment for him.

Heat center Bam Adebayo celebrates with the American flag after USA Basketball won Olympic gold in 2021.

MAX STRUS, THE SIDELINES, AND NBA REPLAY OFFICIALS

THE NBA has an office in Secaucus, New Jersey, called the NBA Replay Center. It's got tons of video screens and the officials there can see every camera angle imaginable in real time as games are being played, which means they're the folks who can really study a replay and see what the right call should be.

And they, for whatever reason, like to check Max Strus's heel placement.

This saga started in Game 7 of the 2022 Eastern Conference Finals, with the Miami Heat taking on the Boston Celtics. Strus made a corner three-pointer early in the second half, only to have it taken away several minutes later by NBA replay officials who said his heel was out of bounds before his shot.

Miami thought it had gotten within 56–54 when Strus rattled in that corner 3 early in the third quarter of Game 7. But the Celtics answered with a 9–1 run, and when the NBA ruling came to take Strus' basket off the board, what had been a 56–54 game became 65–52.

The Heat, after the fact, lamented that those three points were important; the Heat's season ended with a 100–96 loss, though three more points on their side of the scoreboard probably would have had Miami making some different decisions in the final moments of that game.

And in 2023, in a play-in elimination game, Strus had another three-pointer taken away after review in Secaucus. That one didn't matter so much, since Strus scored 31 points and the Heat advanced to Round 1 of the playoffs by beating the Chicago Bulls 102–91.

"They should have given us that one just for the one last year," Heat coach Erik Spoelstra said at the time.

Miami's Max Strus drives past Boston's Marcus Smart during an Eastern Conference finals game.

DUNCAN ROBINSON SETS HEAT THREE-POINT CAREER RECORD

DUNCAN ROBINSON had a path like few others to the NBA. He started his career at Division III's Williams College in Massachusetts before transferring to Michigan.

And he became the most prolific three-point shooter in Miami Heat history.

Career three-pointer No. 807 came for Robinson on December 30, 2022, when the Heat played the Nuggets in Denver. Officially, it was a 27-footer, 28 seconds into the fourth quarter off an assist from Gabe Vincent. It was a swish from the left wing, breaking the mark that had been held by Tim Hardaway.

"For now," Robinson said. "I'm No. 1 for now. . . . I feel very fortunate, blessed to get it."

Robinson got the Heat record in 264 games. Nobody in NBA history ever made 200, 300, 400, 500, 600, 700, 800, 900 and 1,000 three-pointers faster than Robinson did, either.

Not bad for a guy who wasn't drafted, earned a two-way contract with the Heat at first, and kept rising up the charts from there.

And through the end of the 2024–25 season, Robinson was one of only six undrafted players in NBA history with at least 1,200 made threes in his regular-season career.

Heat guard Tyler Herro accepts the 2021–22 NBA Sixth Man of the Year award.

HERRO

THE NBA SIXTH MAN OF THE YEAR

IT WAS before the 2021–22 season, and the Miami Heat had a difficult decision to make. The way they looked at it, they had six players who merited the five spots in the starting lineup.

And in the end, Tyler Herro was the odd man out.

Heat coach Erik Spoelstra has subscribed to the same theories for most of his career. Among them, starting lineups don't matter as much as people think, it's the five players on the floor at the end of games—the closing units—that really matter, and games are won by having your second unit outplay the other team's second unit.

That was why he decided that the Heat would be best served by Herro coming off the bench.

Oh, did it ever work out.

Herro was the 2021–22 NBA Sixth Man of the Year, making him the first player to win the award as a member of the Heat. He averaged 20.7 points, nearly four more per game than any other reserve in the league, and he helped the Heat end up as the No. 1 seed in that season's Eastern Conference playoffs.

"It means a lot," Herro said. "I accepted the sixth-man role for a reason. I wanted to be the best sixth man in the league."

He was, nearly unanimously.

There were 100 sportswriters and broadcasters from around the league who voted for the award; 96 of them put Herro at the top of their sixth-man ballots. It was a runaway.

"Everyone who knows me knows I love Tyler Herro's game (and swag) —much respect on an incredible 6th man campaign," tweeted Cleveland's Kevin Love when the award was announced. (Love would eventually join the Heat.)

Herro's demotion wasn't a demotion. He actually played more minutes that season than anyone else on the Heat.

A PERFECT NIGHT AT THE LINE

HEAT HAD 40-40 VISION

PART OF the beauty of NBA games is that you never know what's going to happen.

Case in point: January 10, 2023. The Miami Heat set an NBA record that night, going 40 for 40 from the foul line, and they needed them all in a 112–111 win over the Oklahoma City Thunder.

Miami's feat that night broke the previous record, a 39-for-39 effort by Utah against Portland on December 7, 1982. And the 40-for-40 game came on a weird night for Miami: The Heat were missing six players because of injuries, four of them starters, and backup center Dewayne Dedmon got ejected for smacking a courtside massage gun with such force that it sailed onto the court.

"It's just a normal Tuesday night for the Miami Heat," Heat coach Erik Spoelstra said.

Jimmy Butler scored 35 points and was 23 for 23 from the line, which tied for the second-most makes without a miss in NBA history. James Harden made 24 without a miss for Houston on December 3, 2019, and when including playoffs, Dirk Nowitzki made 24 without a miss for Dallas in a playoff game against the Thunder on May 17, 2011. The only other player besides Butler with a 23-for-23 game was Dominique Wilkins in 1992.

Jimmy Butler and the Miami Heat made all 40 of their free throws in a game against Oklahoma City in 2023.

Udonis Haslem, in a rocking chair, poses with family before his last regular season game as a Heat player in 2023.

FAREWELL TO THE CAPTAIN

HASLEM SETS A SCORING RECORD IN FINALE

UDONIS HASLEM, the longtime Miami Heat captain, played his final regular season game on April 9, 2023.

It was a legendary show.

He scored 24 points and led the Heat past the Orlando Magic 123–110. But that was just part of the story.

It was Haslem's highest-scoring game in nearly 14 years—he had scored 28 points on November 14, 2009—and he became the first 42-year-old to score 24 or more points in a game. Nobody else in league history, at that time, had been older than 41 years and three days old when scoring at least 24 points; Kareem Abdul-Jabbar had that distinction.

"He is the ultimate competitor, the ultimate teammate, the ultimate winner," Heat coach Erik Spoelstra said of Haslem. "He's about all the right things. He also has that 'it' quality and he's always had that."

It was the third-highest-scoring game of Haslem's career.

"So many people have sacrificed for me and this is for them. This is their day as much as it is mine," Haslem said.

"PLAYOFF JIMMY" STRIKES AGAIN

SCORES 56 IN HEAT WIN OVER BUCKS

JIMMY BUTLER often tried to argue that "Playoff Jimmy" wasn't a thing.

A game against the Milwaukee Bucks in Round 1 of the 2023 Eastern Conference playoffs didn't help his argument.

Butler scored 56 points for the Miami Heat, a franchise playoff record that tied the mark for the second-most points in any game in team history. In the process, Butler led his team back from a 14-point fourth-quarter deficit and to a 119–114 win. The eighth-seeded Heat took a 3–1 lead over the top-seeded Bucks in the series.

"We knew what we were capable of, even if nobody outside of this building, outside of this roster and outside of this organization believed in us," Butler said.

Butler was 19 for 28 from the field and 15 for 18 from the foul line, and he added nine rebounds.

"We deserved to win that game," Heat center Bam Adebayo said, "because he played incredible."

Butler started fast and finished fast. He had 22 points—including 20 straight—in the first quarter, then 21 more in the fourth quarter. His three-pointer with 1:20 left put Miami ahead for good.

It tied the fourth-highest-scoring playoff game in NBA history at the time. Michael Jordan had 63 in 1986, Elgin Baylor had 61 in 1962, and Donovan Mitchell had 57 in 2020. Butler became the fourth with 56, joining Jordan, Wilt Chamberlain, and Charles Barkley.

"Playoff Jimmy" would become Jimmy Butler's alter ego during postseason runs, and he helped Miami reach the 2023 NBA Finals.

2023
MAY 29

BUTLER WINS EASTERN CONFERENCE FINALS MVP

THE 2023 Eastern Conference Finals were unusual, in multiple ways.

A No. 8 seed got to the East finals; the Miami Heat advanced there out of the play-in tournament. That was historic in a good way. And then the Heat nearly did something historic in a not-so-good way.

They won the first three games of the series—then lost the next three. They had to go to Boston and win a Game 7 on the road to avoid becoming the first team in NBA history to blow a 3–0 series lead.

Jimmy Butler said "no problem." He scored 28 points and the Heat rolled to a 103–84 win in Game 7, earning a trip to the NBA Finals.

And Butler got to claim the Larry Bird Trophy—named for the Celtics legend and given to the MVP of the East finals—on Boston's home floor. He won the voting 5–4; Miami's Caleb Martin, who had a sensational East finals, was the runner-up.

It came a year after Miami lost a Game 7 of the 2022 East finals, also at home, also to Boston. Butler vowed after that game that Miami would get back there in 2023.

And he was right.

"I have so much belief in myself and this group of guys, in this squad that Coach Pat (Riley), Spo (Heat coach Erik Spoelstra) and everybody else put together," Butler said. "I see it every single day. I know how good of players that we have and I know how good of a team we are. And we made it happen."

Heat star Jimmy Butler accepts the 2023 Eastern Conference Finals MVP award.

2023
JUNE

THE MIRACLE DOESN'T HAPPEN

EIGHTH-SEEDED HEAT LOSE TO DENVER IN NBA FINALS

IT WOULD have been the most unlikely NBA title in league history.

The Miami Heat were the No. 8 seed coming out of the Eastern Conference in the 2023 NBA playoffs—and made it all the way to the NBA Finals. But in the end, it was the Denver Nuggets and star Nikola Jokic celebrating their first championship. Denver beat the Heat in five games.

And when it was over, Heat coach Erik Spoelstra offered the following words that resonated with fans.

"I think this is a team that a lot of people can relate to," Spoelstra said that night in Denver. "If you ever felt that you were dismissed or felt that you were made to feel less than. We had a lot of people in our locker room that probably have had that, and there's probably a lot of people out there, you know, that have felt that at some time or another.

"But also the way this team handled setbacks and adversity, you know, to develop a collective grit and perseverance. I mentioned this before, that hopefully these are lessons that will transcend this beautiful game. That hopefully these are lessons that we can pass along to our children; that even though it is sport, that you can learn lessons of life from this game. That you can persevere; that you can handle what people may view as mini-failures along the way and become stronger from it and to be able to overcome things and find beautiful things on the other side of that.

"Now, obviously, we didn't get the final win, but sometimes that's true in sport and also in life; that you don't always get what you want. But there's no regret from our side. Everybody, staff, players alike in the locker room put themselves out there and put themselves into the team, whatever was best for the team. And the tough pill to swallow is it just wasn't good enough. We ran up against a team that was just better than us in this series."

Miami's Bam Adebayo tries to defend against Denver star Nikola Jokic. Denver topped Miami in five games for the 2023 NBA title.

WADE TELLS HIS DAD, "WE IN THE HALL OF FAME, DAWG"

DWYANE WADE'S father wasn't always there for him. It was a hard upbringing in Robbins, Illinois, for the future Miami Heat guard. It wasn't easy.

It all worked out, obviously. A three-time champion. An all-time great. An Olympic gold medalist.

And a member of the Basketball Hall of Fame.

Wade's enshrinement speech in Springfield, Massachusetts, had a very special finish. Dwyane Tyrone Wade Jr. brought Dwyane Tyrone Wade Sr. onto the stage and thanked his father for how hard he pushed him at times as a young player, demanding he work on his weaknesses over and over and over again.

"It made me an unstoppable force," Wade told his father, toward the end of his speech. "That time you got kicked out of the game as my coach and snuck back in the side door and coached me from the stands just to get kicked out again. It showed me that there was no limitations on how you would show up for me. It's the exact same way I try to show up for my kids.

"So even though I hated being called Little Dwyane, I admired you as a kid. I admire you. Now, we had the same exact dream and we carry the same exact name, Dwyane Tyrone Wade. To know we hustled all the way to the Basketball Hall of Fame is God's will."

That's when he asked his father to join him on stage, "as we take our rightful step into basketball heaven."

"This one right here, this one is for my father. I love you and I'm thankful for you. . . . We in the Hall of Fame, dawg."

As always, Wade knew how to deliver in crunch time.

Dwyane Wade (right) and his father celebrate the former Heat guard's enshrinement into the Naismith Memorial Basketball Hall of Fame in 2023.

Heat coach Erik Spoelstra led a basketball clinic in Manila during the 2023 Basketball World Cup.

SPO GOES TO MANILA AND EMBRACES HIS ROOTS

TALK ABOUT things falling into place.

The 2023 Basketball World Cup was going to be centered in the Philippines, mostly in Manila. USA Basketball needed assistant coaches to work under Steve Kerr for that tournament and the following year's Paris Olympics. And Miami Heat coach Erik Spoelstra was asked to join that staff.

Which means, at the World Cup, Spoelstra was going to go back to Manila—where he's a huge star.

Let's explain. Spoelstra's mother is from the Philippines. Spoelstra always embraced that part of his heritage, and as he rose to NBA coaching stardom his popularity in the Philippines—a basketball-crazed country—kept rising as well. So in the summer of 2023, Spoelstra finally got to coach for his country while standing on the soil of his mother's homeland.

"I have a great deal of pride in my heritage and I'm close with my family over here," Spoelstra said. "When I first started coming over, I just wanted to give back and do as much as I could, in terms of clinics and continue to grow the game and just be involved in the movement. That's what I call it. Basketball really is like a religion in the Philippines."

One of the first things Spoelstra did after USA Basketball arrived in Manila was lead a clinic for about 40 elite high school and college players, both men's and women's. He desperately wants to be part of growing the game there.

"I never played in the (Philippines Basketball Association) like I wanted, but I ended up getting to share the game in a different way," Spoelstra said. "And that's a beautiful thing as well. It didn't need to be me playing. It worked with me going back and giving back and still getting to do this."

Jimmy Butler arrived for media day entering the 2023–24 season in character as "Emo Jimmy."

THE DEBUT OF "EMO JIMMY"

MEDIA DAY in the NBA—usually the day before the first practice of training camp—is always an unusual day. Some players are wearing the uniforms of their new team for the first time. Others might be talking about championship expectations or the offseason departure of past teammates or coaches. You never know what's coming.

And then there was Miami Heat media day 2023.

That was the day that "Emo Jimmy" stole the NBA's headlines.

Jimmy Butler had a new look for media day that year. He arrived for the team's first official day of work that season with piercings—eye, lip and nose, all of it faked—along with a new hairstyle and his fingernails painted black.

"I'm very emotional right now. This is my emo state and I like this. This is me," Butler said. "This is how I'm feeling as of late."

Bam Adebayo saw a picture of "Emo Jimmy" before seeing Butler for real, and thought the image was photoshopped. Tyler Herro thought Butler was just dressing up early for Halloween.

But Butler knew exactly what he was doing. His official season headshot was taken that day. And that meant, on TV for much of the year, if you saw a Butler graphic, you probably saw a photo of "Emo Jimmy."

SPO GETS RICHEST CONTRACT FOR A COACH IN NBA HISTORY

HE CAME to the Miami Heat in 1995 for a job in the video room. He was promoted to head coach in 2008. And in 2024, Erik Spoelstra set a record by signing what at that time was the richest coaching contract in NBA history in terms of total salary.

The Heat locked up Spoelstra on an eight-year, $120 million deal. It came with only a few months left on the contract that Spoelstra was coaching under, but nobody ever thought he would leave Miami.

The team didn't think so either—but the contract ensured that he isn't going anywhere.

At the time, Spoelstra was the league's second-longest-tenured current coach behind San Antonio's Gregg Popovich.

"We're about the sweat and the grind," Spoelstra said before the 2023–24 season. "It's about when nobody's watching. We have a saying at the Heat: 'There's a beauty in the grind, there's a beauty in the sweat.' That's about what happens behind the scenes."

Spoelstra, clearly, was on a Hall of Fame path. He led the Heat on a 27-game winning streak on the way to a 66–16 record in the 2012–13 season, and the winning streak was the second-longest ever in the NBA—six games shy of the 33-game run by the Los Angeles Lakers in the early 1970s. Spoelstra also coached the Heat to the 2012 and 2013 NBA titles with the teams led by LeBron James, Dwyane Wade, and Chris Bosh.

"We've had incredible stability and consistency over the years," Spoelstra once said when asked about how he's remained with the Heat for so long. "I've been very fortunate to work for who I work for."

Erik Spoelstra is Miami's all-time leader in coaching wins.

HEAT RETIRE HASLEM'S NUMBER

IF YOU'RE not a Miami Heat fan, you probably don't understand this.

The player we're talking about here was never an All-Star. He never was a max-contract player. Never won a player of the week award, and he was in the league for 20 years. He averaged 7.5 points and 6.6 rebounds. He barely played for the last few years of his time on the active roster.

Given those stats, it doesn't sound like the person had a lot of star power.

But in this case, we're talking about Udonis Haslem. And numbers be damned, he was a Heat legend.

The Heat retired his jersey number 40 in January 2024, the end of a career where he was undrafted and became unforgettable.

Only two other players—Dallas's Dirk Nowitzki and the Los Angeles Lakers' Kobe Bryant—had a career of 20 years or more and only played for one franchise in that span.

"You all got the money on me crying, don't y'all? I know you all think I'm going to cry," Haslem said as the jersey was raised, and the tough-as-nails son of Miami stopped to wipe tears from his eyes. "Yeah, it's hard. It's hard. It's hard. Heat Nation, it's been an absolute honor, man."

Haslem was the sixth player to get a jersey retired by the Heat. The others: Chris Bosh (No 1), Dwyane Wade (No. 3), Tim Hardaway (No. 10), Shaquille O'Neal (No. 32), and Alonzo Mourning (No. 33).

"Udonis Haslem, his force mattered and it counted," Heat President Pat Riley said on the jersey-retirement night. "And that's one of the reasons why we're hanging his jersey here today. . . . Udonis Haslem is going to leave a very big footprint." Haslem was hired as Miami's vice president of player programs going into the 2023-24 season.

A HEAT-RECORD 60-POINT WIN

WHEN THE game was over on March 29, 2024, Miami Heat center Bam Adebayo looked at the stat sheet and was just befuddled by what he was reading.

"One of those fun nights," he said.

Oh, it was fun for the Heat that night—the most one-sided win in team history.

Final score: Heat 142, Portland Trail Blazers 82. The 60-point margin was the biggest ever by a Miami team, coming in a game in which just about everyone got into the scoring act. Thomas Bryant scored 26 points, Terry Rozier scored 22, Adebayo had 21 (and was one assist away from a triple-double), Haywood Highsmith scored 20, Patty Mills scored 17, and Jaime Jaquez Jr. finished with 12.

Jimmy Butler had only eight that night, and took only four shots. Obviously, that didn't matter.

And the Heat won every quarter by at least 10 points. Nikola Jovic either scored or assisted on each of Miami's first four baskets of the second half, then got the rest of the night off to watch and enjoy.

"Things started going our way," Adebayo said, when asked afterward how to explain such a night, "and I guess they kept going our way."

Simple enough.

Nikola Jovic and the Heat won a game over Portland by 60 points during the 2023–24 season.

LIONEL MESSI STOPS BY A HEAT GAME

THE REALLY good tickets are hard to get for Miami Heat games. Getting a bunch of them, for a playoff game, on almost no notice . . . well, that's tough for anyone to pull off.

That is, unless you're Lionel Messi.

He decided he wanted to bring a few friends to watch a Heat–Boston Celtics playoff game, and naturally, the Heat found a way to make it happen. Messi, the star from Inter Miami of Major League Soccer and the eight-time Ballon d'Or winner as soccer's best player, showed up for that game with teammates Jordi Alba, Sergio Busquets, and Luis Suarez.

They arrived just before tip-off (hey, it's Miami, everyone comes late) and parked in the part of the garage reserved for players, team employees, and VIPs. Some members of Messi's group wore Heat attire; Busquets wore a Heat hooded sweatshirt.

If they were Heat fans that night, they left disappointed. Miami lost Game 4 of that first-round series to Boston, then was eliminated in Game 5—so Messi saw the final home game of that 2023–24 season.

Inter Miami stars Lionel Messi (left) and Sergio Busquets (right) watch a Heat game late in the 2023–24 season.

Heat President Pat Riley speaks at the ceremony renaming the team's home floor in his honor in 2024.

WELCOME TO PAT RILEY COURT

PAT RILEY didn't want the court that the Miami Heat call home to bear his name.

Most people might not have realized that. As President, Pat Riley runs the Heat, right? He makes the decisions. He's the boss. Ordinarily, yes, that is correct.

But not in 2024. Riley has a boss. And Heat Managing General Partner Micky Arison—along with his son Nick Arison, the Heat CEO—had a plan for the court.

Riley was getting what in their minds was a long-overdue honor.

"Enjoy it," Micky Arison told Riley. "It's going to be there forever."

The ceremony was at the 2024–25 home opener, with 20,000 fans in attendance. Fans tend to leave their seats at halftime in most arenas, Miami included. But on this night, far more than usual stayed put to watch the Riley celebration.

"It will end here one day. And that stamp here and that stamp over there, that's what it's all about, sweetie," Riley said that night during his speech, directing his remarks to his wife Chris and pointing to the two spots on the court that now bear his signature and name. "We made it. We made it. I love you. Thank you."

Among the former players in attendance: Dwyane Wade, Goran Dragic, Mike Miller, and Jamal Mashburn.

"This is beyond even my imagination of a reward for a man's life's work," Riley said. "We are huge dreamers and Micky has made mine. It wasn't something I wanted or pursued, but I'm going to take it."

WADE GETS A STATUE, AND CRITICISM

HERE'S SOMETHING to clear up: No, the statue does not exactly look like Dwyane Wade's face.

There's a statue, the first ever commissioned by the Miami Heat, outside their arena, the Kaseya Center. It was unveiled in 2024 to honor Wade's role as the face of the franchise for many years. It was immediately panned by fans and critics alike because it, well, doesn't exactly look like the Heat's all-time scoring leader.

(OK, it doesn't look anything like him.)

Wade doesn't adhere to a lot of norms. He's always taken risks in fashion, for example. He likes being different. He likes being something that people don't immediately understand, and he likes being a talking point for those people.

Which brings us back to the statue. To hear him tell the story, it wasn't supposed to look like him.

"If I wanted it to look like me, I'd just stand outside the arena and y'all can take photos," Wade said. "It don't need to look like me. It's the artistic version of a moment that happened that we're trying to cement."

The moment was when the Heat beat the Chicago Bulls in March 2009, a game where Wade made a running jumper to win at the buzzer of double overtime, hopped up onto a courtside table and yelled, "This is my house."

The statue's body sort of looks like him in that moment.

The face, not so much.

"I care, but I don't," Wade said. "The social media world is about opinions. Everyone has an opinion. Everyone, use y'all opinions. Please talk more about us. Talk more about a statue, come on down to see it, take some photos, send some memes. We don't care."

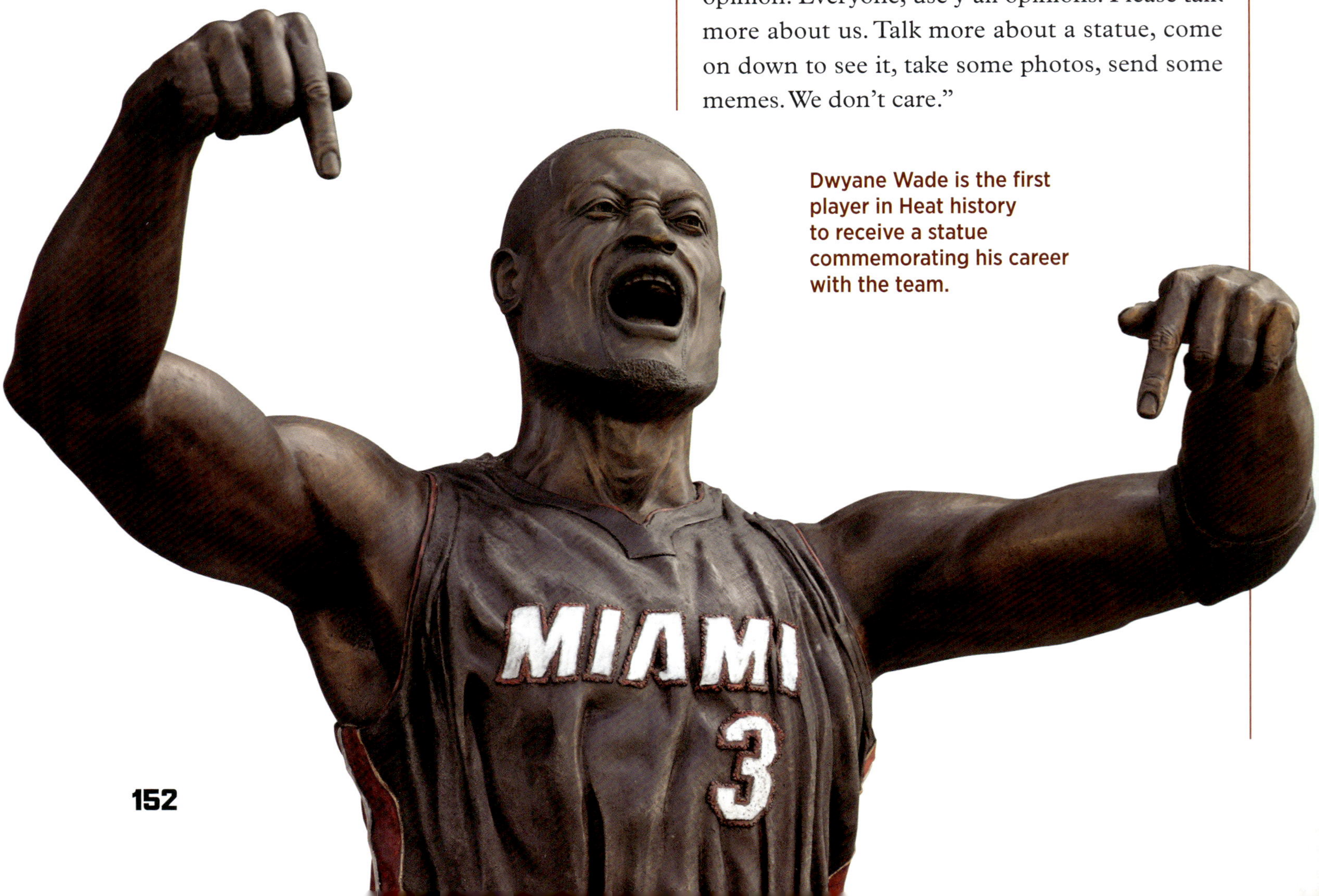

Dwyane Wade is the first player in Heat history to receive a statue commemorating his career with the team.

ADEBAYO'S OLYMPIC BANNER (PART 2)

BAM ADEBAYO knew what was coming. He went through it in 2021. And in 2024, he got his second Olympic gold-medal commemorative banner from the Miami Heat.

With sneakers that were trimmed in gold—fittingly, given the hue of the medal that he and USA Basketball had won at the Paris Olympics earlier that year—Adebayo and his mother Marilyn Blount were at midcourt to watch his second Olympic banner unveiled. Heat coach Erik Spoelstra, an assistant on that US team that beat France for a fifth consecutive gold medal, was part of the ceremony as well.

Adebayo's mother wore the gold medal from the Tokyo Games. She draped the one from the Paris Games over her son's shoulders for the big moment.

"Keep tallying them up," said Adebayo, who became the first player to win two Olympic gold medals while playing for the Heat. "Obviously, it's something special. It keeps marking my name in the history books."

Adebayo became the first player to win two Olympic gold medals while active with the Heat. The Heat started the banner tribute in 2008 after Dwyane Wade was part of the "Redeem Team" squad that won at the Beijing Games. The Heat raised retroactive ones not long afterward for Tim Hardaway and Alonzo Mourning—teammates on the team that won at the Sydney Games in 2000. Another banner hangs for LeBron James, who won gold for the US at London in 2012 when he was with the Heat.

Bam Adebayo rises for a dunk during the 2024 Paris Olympics, when he won his second gold medal with USA Basketball.

Heat forward-center Kevin Love spent much of his time in Miami reaching out to schools and speaking on the importance of mental health.

THE FEARLESSNESS OF KEVIN LOVE

AND HIS PURSUIT OF HELPING OTHERS

KEVIN LOVE came to the Miami Heat in 2023 because the team knew he had plenty left as a player.

He gave them much more.

Love won an NBA title with Cleveland in 2016, was a lottery pick, surely will end up in the Basketball Hall of Fame one day, and was a bona fide star for a long time in this league. And for years, Love fought a silent battle with anxiety—before he was in the first group of players, alongside DeMar DeRozan, to decide that it would be OK to discuss those struggles openly in hopes of helping others with their mental health.

Love reached out to students in South Florida, bringing groups to the arena for events and visiting schools, too. He talked with teammates. He would talk with anybody, really. He was unafraid to share, and that made others unafraid to talk.

"Teammates trusting me and allowing me to be unapologetically myself allowed me to be more comfortable in my own skin and actually able to breathe better out there on the floor," Love said. "Sharing your story, you might change your own life. You might change the next person's life. It's an amazing thing."

He started the Kevin Love Fund to help provide resources that people—especially kids—need. It was, as he likes to say, bigger than basketball.

"It's a beautiful thing to see where this is heading," Love said.

HERRO

THE NBA'S THREE-POINT KING AT ALL-STAR WEEKEND

THROUGH 2025, no team has owned the NBA's three-point contest at All-Star Weekend like the Miami Heat.

And Tyler Herro added his name to the list of shootout champions that year.

The Heat became the first franchise to have players win five All-Star three-point contests, with Herro adding himself to a club that already included Glen Rice in 1995, Jason Kapono in 2007, Daequan Cook in 2009, and James Jones in 2011. They all won the contest as members of the Heat.

"It means a lot," Herro said that night. "I feel like a lot of great shooters, a lot of great players, some of the greats to play this game have won this award—not award, this competition. Just happy to put my name in the history books for All-Star Weekend."

Herro won the competition in San Francisco, one night before he played in his first All-Star Game.

"This weekend has obviously meant a lot to me," he said when it was over, before heading back to Miami. "I know I'm never going to forget it."

Heat guard Tyler Herro poses with the trophy after winning the three-point contest at the NBA's All-Star weekend in 2025.

THE BUTLER ERA ENDS

IN THE end, it had to happen. The Miami Heat knew it. Jimmy Butler knew it. And after a weeks-long standoff because he was unhappy with his role, in February 2025, the trade went down.

Butler left Miami without a championship. The team went to the NBA Finals twice in his time in Miami, but never won a title.

The Heat traded Butler primarily for Andrew Wiggins. It was a very bad breakup—including three suspensions in January 2025, an infamous comment from Butler about how he lost his joy, and his bristling from criticism that came his way from Heat President Pat Riley months earlier.

"I know I have my joy back now," Butler said.

He took the high road when leaving the organization, not taking any unnecessary shots on his way out of Miami.

"I don't got too many bad things to say about them," Butler said. "I don't. They gave me opportunity. I felt like I did my job to the highest level. I have so much respect for that organization, for the people that's running that organization and for my former teammates. And I'm always going to wish them the best."

Butler came to Miami in 2019 and immediately took Dwyane Wade's spot as the star of the team—he even got Wade's locker in the Miami locker room. Butler was a two-time All-Star with the Heat and had eight 40-point playoff games—earning the moniker "Playoff Jimmy."

"It's all good," Butler said.

Jimmy Butler was traded by the Miami Heat to the Golden State Warriors in 2025.

MICKY ARISON MAKES THE HALL OF FAME

MICKY ARISON doesn't like the term "owner." Around the Miami Heat—the team that, yes, he owns—his official title is managing general partner.

In 2025, he got another title: Basketball Hall of Famer.

Arison was selected to the Hall's class alongside the 2008 US Olympic men's basketball "Redeem Team" plus Carmelo Anthony, Dwight Howard, Sue Bird, Maya Moore, Sylvia Fowles, Billy Donovan, and Danny Crawford.

Arison's father, Ted Arison, was instrumental in Miami getting a franchise. But it wasn't until 1995 that Micky Arison took control of the team.

"I went out and got some of the best people I could, starting with Pat Riley, and they took it from there," Arison said. "To me, this is an award and a recognition of the efforts of the organization, the Miami Heat organization, all its employees, and especially its great players that we've had over the last 30 years."

Arison said he has a simple managerial style, one that has paid off with three championships, seven trips to the NBA Finals, and the league's third-best record over his first 30 years at the controls.

"Come to work on time, work hard, be proud in what you're accomplishing, support your teammates," Arison said. "We talk about enjoying each other's successes. And that's what it's all about."

Retired Duke coach Mike Krzyzewski talks with Heat Managing General Partner Micky Arison after the Naismith Memorial Basketball Hall of Fame class was announced in 2025.

Tyler Herro and the Miami Heat were all smiles after 11 players scored at least nine points in a win over New Orleans in 2025.

YOU NEVER KNOW WHEN A RECORD WILL GET SET

THE MIAMI Heat were playing out the string of the 2024–25 season. They were going to the play-in tournament no matter what, and the 81st game of that season was one that looked meaningless in New Orleans against the Pelicans.

Surprise!

The Heat did something that night that no team in NBA history had previously managed.

Miami beat New Orleans 153–104. Bam Adebayo scored 23 points, Tyler Herro scored 22, Duncan Robinson scored 21, Alec Burks scored 12, Jaime Jaquez Jr. and Davion Mitchell each scored 11, Andrew Wiggins scored 10, Kel'el Ware scored 10, Haywood Highsmith scored 10, Keshad Johnson scored 10, and Kyle Anderson scored nine.

What did all that mean?

That was the first time in the NBA's 78-season history that 11 different players from one team scored at least nine points in the same game.

THE SELLOUT STREAK

THERE ARE a few undeniable truths about Miami Heat fans. Most of them do not show up on time; there are a variety of reasons for that, traffic being a very real one of them, though even on weekends people tend to arrive late for tip-off.

And some of them typically leave games early. It happens everywhere, though Miami fans tend to take the most heat for it, no pun intended.

But they do show up. Often late, sure, but they do show up.

Which brings us to the streak of Miami Heat sellouts—15 years and counting.

Going back to late in the 2010 season, the Heat have announced a sellout at every single regular season and postseason game. That's 640 in all, going into the 2025 playoffs. Sometime in the 2025–26 season, the Heat could have the third-longest sellout streak in NBA history. Boston sold out 662 consecutive games from 1980 through 1995.

Dallas (which went over the 1,000-game mark in the 2024–25 season) and Portland (814 straight from 1977 through 1995) are the only teams with longer streaks than that run of Celtics games and now, this run of Heat games.

The Miami Heat have one of the longest streaks of sold-out games in NBA history.

SOURCES

ABC/ESPN

ASAP Sports, asapsports.com

Associated Press archive, apnews.com

Basketball Reference, basketball-reference.com

Getty Images

Miami Heat

Miami Heat media guides, 1988–2024

Miami Herald archives

NBA, nba.com

NBA Entertainment

Newspapers.com

Official NBA register, 1988–2024

Palm Beach Post archives

South Florida Sun-Sentinel archives

Sportradar, radar360.sportradar.com

Shaquille O'Neal's arrival sparked Miami's first championship run in 2006.